AF335508

A layman's guide to

ALEXANDER
THE
GREAT

A layman's guide to

ALEXANDER
THE
GREAT

by

MAUREEN CARTER

EFSTATHIADIS GROUP

Efstathiadis Group S.A.
Agiou Athanasiou Street,
GR-145 65 Anixi, Attikis

ISBN 960 226 556 6

© Efstathiadis Group S.A. 1996

All rights reserved; no part of this
publication may be reproduced, stored in a
retrieval system or transmitted, in any form
or by any means, electronic, mechanical,
photocopying, recording, or otherwise, without the
prior permission of Efstathiadis Group S.A.

Printed and bound in Greece by Efstathiadis Group S.A.

*To my husband, Alan. Without his
expertise in the kitchen, this book
would never have been written.*

"All the business of war, and indeed all the business of
life, is to endeavour to find out what you don't know by
what you do; that's what I call 'guessing what was at
the other side of the hill ' ".

*The Duke of Wellington
The Croker Papers
1875*

List of Illustrations

List of Maps

Contents

An old proverb long ago be said,
That oft the son in manners like will be unto his father.

INTRODUCTION

I have begun this account of Alexander the Great with a brief look at his father, Philip of Macedon. Without detracting from the achievements of Alexander, we must recognise that he was the son of a great leader, and a clever, crafty diplomat. Like many great men before and after him, Philip worked hard and played hard. He was a philanderer, many times married and he drank too much. But he was an inspirational and courageous soldier, fair and compassionate in victory and injured many times in battle, losing his right eye from an arrow wound.

In 1977, a Greek professor, Manolis Andronikos, when digging behind a ruined tomb at Vergina, in Greek Macedonia, discovered two more graves, almost intact. One contained the remains of a young boy, identified as the son of Alexander the Great. The child was murdered when he was thirteen. The other grave was most probably that of the half brother of Alexander and many believe that Philip of Macedon was buried in the first tomb. Bone fragments found there, when pieced together, show a skull with a damaged right eye socket.

But where is Alexander's tomb? He had requested to be buried at Siwa, where he had visited the temple to Zeus Ammon and where the priests had hailed him as son of Zeus. History has it, though, that his remains were taken from Babylon to Memphis and from there to Alexandria. Famous people were said to have paid their respects at his tomb in Alexandria, yet it has never been found.

Recently, a Greek archaeologist, Lianna Souvaltzi, digging at a burial site at Siwa, not far from the ruins of the temple of Ammon, came across the remains of three tablets, inscribed in Greek. The script carved into the stone indicates that Alexander could have been brought to Siwa and Souvaltzi is convinced that she has found Alexander's tomb. Others are sceptical. Work has ceased for the time being, until the authorities give permission for continued excavation.

 Most of the manuscripts concerning Alexander, written during and just after his lifetime, have been lost. Only fragments, mostly illegible, remain. Between three and five hundred years after his death, five works, including one by the Greek biographer, Plutarch, were written based on these manuscripts. Many learned histories of Alexander have been written by modern day scholars using these second hand accounts. Using both the old and modern texts I have tried to give an easy to read account of Alexander and his achievements. In striving for accuracy yet simplicity I have avoided, as far as possible, politics and detailed descriptions of battles. This work is intended to whet the appetite. For those who want to know more, I have included a short bibliography at the back of the book.

Part 1

The Father

PHILIP II OF MACEDON

Times of war often produce great men and, during the Peloponnesian wars, a great general emerged in Thebes. His name was Epaminondas. When faced with the Spartan army at the Battle of Leuktra, in 371 BC, he employed a new tactic. Behind his cavalry, which, as was normal, faced the enemy cavalry, he massed his Theban infantry, in a phalanx fifty deep, to consitute his left wing. He himself advanced in a slanting line towards the left. While the Spartans formed a new front, his Boeotian cavalry charged and broke through enemy lines.

Between this battle and the Battle of Mantinea in 362 BC, where Epaminondas used the same tactics, a young man from Macedonia had been held hostage in Thebes for three years. His name was Philip and he took a great interest in the affairs of Thebes and her military.

Epaminondas was mortally wounded at Mantinea, although he had broken, once more, through the enemy lines. The battle, which marked the end of the Peloponnesian wars, ended in a draw. The Athenian, Xenophon, wrote that there was even more confusion and chaos in Greece after the battle than before. It was a fruit ripe for the picking and young Philip, released and back in Macedonia, was soon in a position to pluck it when, in 360 BC, he became King of Macedonia. His brother, King Perdicaas III, had been killed in a battle against the Illyrians who held sway over his northern territories.

Macedon was considered by the Greeks to be a country of wild barbarians. Its origins lay way back in that misty time between myth and history when Prometheus stole fire from the gods. Zeus, in his anger, sent a flood to destroy the human race. Prometheus warned his son, Deucalion who, with his wife Pyrrha, built an ark and the pair survived the deluge. When the waters receeded, Deucalion and Pyrrha, obeying the Oracle at the place which later became Delphi, threw stones over their shoulders. Those that Deucalion threw became men and those that Pyrrah threw became women. Thus the human race was restored.

Deucalion and Pyrrah had a son, Hellen, the founder of the Hellenic peoples. Hellen, according to the Greek poet and historian, Hesiod, had three sons and a daughter. The daughter, Thyia, had two sons by Zeus, namely Magnes and Macedon, who lived in the area around Olympus and Pieria. The Magnesians were driven out of their lands but the Macedons remained, becoming isolated, geographically, from their neighbours. They formed a tribal state, taking their kings from one royal tribe, until a certain Perdicaas, a refugee from Argos, on the Peloponnese, took the throne, circa 650 BC. He claimed to be a descendant of the god Zeus through Heracles and that Hero's grandson, Temenus.[1]

---

[1] When Heracles died, his son, Hyllos, consulted the Oracle at Delphi, to discover how he and his brothes might claim back their father's inheritance. The Oracle told them to wait for the third fruit. Hyllos misunderstood the Oracle, waited for the third harvest and went to war, but was killed. The Oracle had meant the third generation and Temenus and his cousins eventually conquered the Peloponnese. They drew lots for territory and Temenus won Argos.

Perdicaas and his heirs called themselves Temenidae and ruled Macedonia for three centuries.

Although the Macedonians spoke Greek, their dialect was such that the Greeks could not understand them. A century before Philip came to power, Herodotus had said: "There is our Hellenism, our being of the same stock and the same speech, our common stories of the gods and rituals, our similar customs." The Greeks, unable to understand the Macedon speech, considered the Macedonians to be not Hellenes but foreign and all foreigners were barbarians. When young Philip took the throne, in the year 359 BC, at the age of twenty three, one of his first actions was against the Illyrians who had killed his brother. Using the tactics of Epaminondas, learned as a young hostage in Thebes, victory was his. Within the first four years of his reign Philip, needing access to the sea, had taken several coastal towns in and around his kingdom, including Amphipolis, which had been settled by Greeks. He also commanded the gold and silver mines around Mount Pangaeum. The wealth from these he used to equip and train a strong and permanent Macedonian army, his small landowners providing the infantry, or Foot Companions, which formed the Macedonian Phalanx, a variation of that of Epaminondas, the men armed with a new weapon, the "sarissa", a pike sometimes as long as six yards. The larger landowners, the "King's Companions," provided well equipped cavalry units. The infantry were taught to form a tight shield to shield defence, copied by Philip from the tactics of an Athenian genereal, Charidemus. This general was later banished from Athens by Alexander.

In the year 357, Philip married Olympias, a wild woman from Molossi, in Epirus and the next year she provided him with a son, Alexander. Molossi took its name from a character from antiquity, Molossus, son of Hermione and Neoptolemus, the latter being a son of Achilles, the central figure in Homer's Iliad. Achilles, the star of Homer's Iliad, was the young Alexander's hero and he was reputed to have slept always with the book under his pillow. His other hero was his ancestor, Heracles and when, in later years, he went into battle, his helmet was carved in the likeness of the lion's head which that hero donned after he killed the Nemean Lion as one of his labours.

Some of the wealth from Philip's gold mines went to enriching the court. Painters came, sculptors, doctors and wise men, many from foreign and exotic lands. An exiled Persian, one Artabazus, arrived with his beautiful young daughter, Barsine. Possibly it was from him that the young Alexander learned to speak Persian.

In 343 the great Greek philosopher, Aristotle, was living near the Macedonian capital and he became tutor to the thirteen year old Prince Alexander. Although some dispute this fact, when Alexander died and there was anti-Macedonian feeling in Greece, Aristotle, who was then director of the Lyceum he had founded in Athens, was forced to flee that city and he died a year later in Chalcis.

Meanwhile, Philip extended his power into Thessaly and Chalcidice fell to him. Soon he was Guardian of the holy Sanctuary of Apollo at Delphi. He planned to unite the whole of Greece under his rule. But first he looked to an old enemy, Persia.

When had Persia become a threat to Greece? The answer begins way back in time, about 1100 BC, when the Dorians invaded Greece from the north. The populace fled in several directions and some found their way to the west coast of Asia Minor, where they established cities. Around the mid

1. *Heracles in the lion skin.*

seventh century BC, the rulers of Lydia came into conflict with these cities which were finally subjugated by King Croesus, in the mid sixth century BC. Croesus, who ruled from Sardis, was fabulously wealthy and was much liked by the Greeks.   He, in turn, enjoyed Greek culture, donated treasure to Delphi and restored the great temple of Artemis at Ephesus.

But in 546 BC, the ruler of the Achaemenid Empire, Cyrus the Great, defeated King Croesus in battle at Sardis and the Greeks of Asia Minor gradually came under Persian rule.

These cities, aided by Athens, revolted against their masters around 490 BC, but the rebellion was crushed and the Persian ruler of the time, Darius I, invaded Thrace and Amynctas, ruler of Macedon, became his vassal. The Persian wars had begun.

Darius I was routed by the Athenian army at the battle of Marathon and ten years later, the Persian king, Xerxes, invaded once more. Alexander I ruled Macedon at the time and he sided with Xerxes, but later said that he gave aid to Greece in secret. (This is probably true, for subsequently the king was accepted as a Greek at Olympia during the Games and the poet Pindar sang his praises.) Xerxes took Athens and burned it, but his fleet was defeated at the battle of Salamis and he retreated with his army to Asia Minor.

So Persia had long regarded Greece as her own and Philip knew that until he had first conquered her, he would never dominate the Greeks. Meanwhile, she was using her great wealth to stir up feelings against Macedonia.

Some Athenians, a certain Isocrates among them, saw Macedonia as a Greek power and preferred to be allied to Philip, (who, they felt, posed no threat to Athens) than to kneel to the savage Persians. Others, however, led by

Demosthenes, a great Athenian orator, saw Macedonia as an immediate threat. With the help of Persian money they would overcome her and, afterwards they could defeat the Persian armies as they had done in the past.

Foreseeing the collapse of the city states under Macedonian rule, Demosthenes ranted long and hard against Philip and the barbaric Macedonians. To the Athenians, who were tired and apathetic after years of war, he spoke thus:

"Philip is not a man to rest satisfied with conquests won, he is ever enlarging his circle and, whilst we wait and fold our hands, he envelops us on all sides with his toils. When, when, Athenians, will you do your duty? What are you waiting for? For necessity?.........Or tell me, do you prefer to stroll about and ask one another, is there any news? Why, what newer thing could there be than a Macedonian subjugating Athenians and ordering the affairs of Greece?"

In 339 BC, Philip marched south as far as Elateia and the Athenians at last became alarmed. Demosthenes went to Thebes to patch up old quarrels and, in 338, the combined might of Athens and Thebes met Philip and his experienced army on the battle-field at Chaeronea, in Boeotia. Once again the great Macedonian Phalanx won the day. The cavalry charge which broke through the enemy lines was led by a nineteen year old prince, Philip's son, Alexander.

Isokrates, who had always hoped to see Greece co-operate with Macedonia in a great war against Persia under Philip's leadership, but not as a subject state, killed himself on hearing of the Greek defeat.

Philip buried his dead, released the Athenian prisoners and sent Alexander to escort home the ashes of the Athenian dead. He summoned a conference of the Panhellenic League which met at Corinth and established peace between the city states. Then, in 337, he was ready at last to declare war against Persia and sent his great general, Parmenion, into Asia as his advance guard.

Alas, Philip was doomed never to achieve his goal. He was assassinated in 336 BC while attending the marriage feast of his daughter. The assassin, a certain Pausanias, one of his bodyguards, was put to death at once, but it is not known whether he acted alone or on the orders of another. Some say that Philip's wife, Olympias, mother of Alexander, saw the birth of a child to Philip's newest young wife, Cleopatra, as a threat to her own son and was behind the deed. However, it has never been suggested, even by his enemies, that the young Alexander was involved.

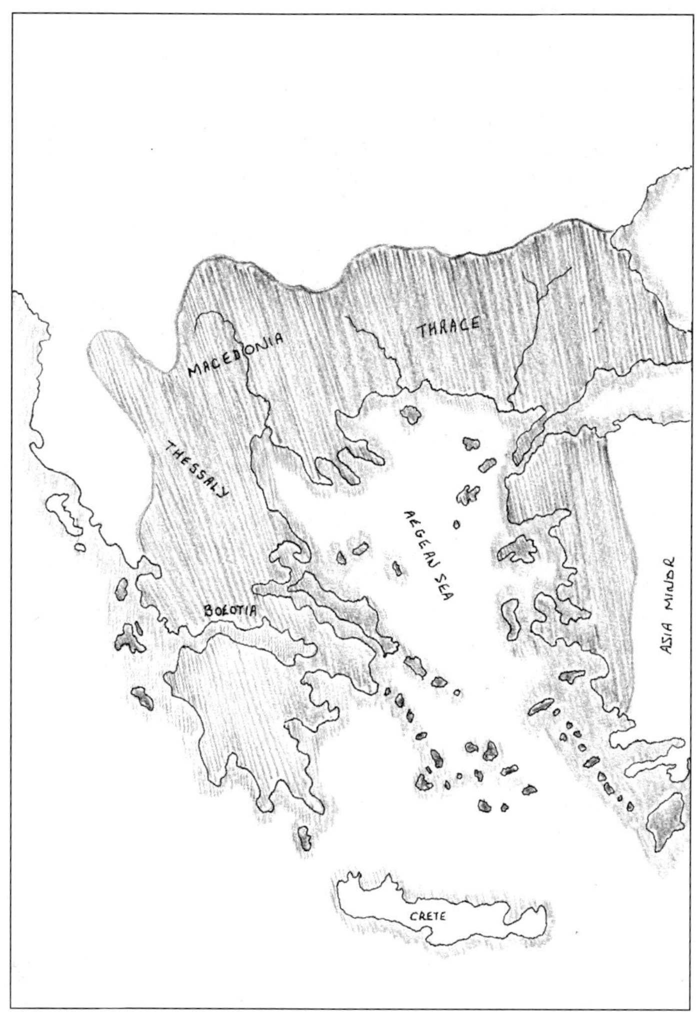

Map 1   *Land ruled by Philip of Macedon II*

Part 2

The Son

THE GREAT ALEXANDER

Long ago, before history was recorded and according to an old legend, a poor peasant of Phrygia, a certain Gordius, saw an eagle alight on his oxcart. When it showed no desire to move, Gordius thought that it was a sign from the gods. He drove the cart, together with the motionless bird, to Telmissus, a part of Phrygia where there was an oracle. As he neared the place, a young prophetess appeared and told him that he had to offer sacrifice to the great Zeus before consulting the oracle. Gordius, struck by her beauty, asked her to marry him after the sacrifice and she consented. Meanwhile, the king of Phrygia died and as he had no heirs, the people asked the oracle who should take the throne. The priestess told them that their new king was approaching, in an ox cart, with his bride.

As Gordius and his bride entered the town, the people crowded round, acclaiming him king and marvelling at the eagle. In thanks to Zeus, Gordius dedicated his cart to the god, tying it to the yoke with a complicated knot. Then the oracle spoke once more. Whoever untied the knot, it stated, would be ruler of all Asia. Many tried, but none were successful.

Gordius founded a city named Gordium where the cart and yoke were guarded by the priests of Zeus. Centuries passed until a young king came to Gordium and heard of the oracle.

Unable to untie the complicated knot, he impetuously took his sword and cut it. His name was Alexander.

Impetuous he was. Brave, reckless, daring, vain, cruel, charming, irascible, magnanimous, all these he was as well and, at times of greatest danger, the Greek goddess of fortune, Tyche or, as some would call her, Lady Luck, seemed to be at his side. Perhaps for that reason he thought he was divine. He was Alexander the Great.

What did he look like? We have seen his face in sculptures and on mosaics, but these are probably idealised. We do know that he was fair skinned and had a thick mane of fair hair, worn longer than was fashionable at the time, swept back from his forehead. In the myths and legends that were told after his death, his hair was likened to a lion's mane. He was clean shaven and rumour has it that he was short in stature. The intensity of his gaze was compelling and added to his charisma. He had a liking for aromatic oils and ointments so always smelled sweet.

Like most royal princes, Alexander did not have a normal childhood. His father spent years away from home on his campaigns and his mother, Olympias, apart from enjoying the company of snakes, indulged in the wild worship of the god of wine, Dionysus. When Philip rejected Olympias, though, Alexander took his mother's side and when Philip married Cleopatra, a toast was made at the wedding feast which implied that Alexander was not legitimate. The prince understandably lost his temper, Philip drew his sword but luckily was the worse for drink and the blow was never struck. Alexander left the court and joined his mother in Epirus for a while, but became reconciled to his father once more and returned to the royal household. He had gathered around himself a close circle of friends of his own age and sex and among these were Harpalus and Nearchus along with Ptolemy. The Macedonians believed that Ptolemy was Philip's son, Alexander's half brother and a story goes that Philip had given the pregnant mother to a man called Lagos. But Hephaestion was Alexander's most beloved friend.

Ancient Greeks accepted a degree of homosexuality as normal. It was fashionable for older men to admire the vigour and beauty of youth. Aristotle, remember he was Alexander's tutor, said:

"Lovers look at none of the bodily charms of their favourites more than at their eyes, wherein dwells the secret of boyish virtues."

Hephaestion, we do not know his age, was Alexander's lover, but the young king was also to have mistresses and at least one wife.

Alexander had a passion for hunting and horses. He loved poetry, music and lite-

2.

Achilles drags Hector behind his chariot.

rature, enjoying the plays of Euripedes and Aeschylus. He read and admired Xenophon, the Greek historian and soldier. Xenophon, in 401 BC, had become a mercenary in the service of Cyrus, the brother of Ataxerxces the Persian king. When Cyrus was killed at Cunaxa, near Babylon, Xenophon led ten thousand Greeks home, across 1,000 miles of enemy territory, along the Euphrates, to the Black Sea and on to the the Aegean shores. An exciting story to inspire a young prince whose other hero, Achilles, was, at the tender age of fifteen, Admiral of the Greek fleet which sailed for Troy and ten years of war.

Achilles distinguished himself in battle and, like Alexander after him, had a lover, Patroclus. When Patroclus was killed by Hector, Achilles took his revenge, slaying many Trojans until he reached and killed Hector who stood alone beneath the walls of Troy. Achilles stripped the body, tied it to the back of his chariot and dragged it around the city until the Trojan king begged him to stop. Such was his rage and grief. And these were the heroes of the twenty year old youth who became King of Macedon in 336 BC.

Alexander's first action on acceeding the throne was to rid himself of those who had plotted against his father. Three brothers were involved and two were put to death, Alexander Lyncestes being spared as he had immediately, on Philip's death, hailed Alexander as king and because he was Antipater's son in law. Antipater was a senior army commander and a friend of Alexander's tutor, Aristotle. Attalus, the uncle of Philip's last wife, Cleopatra, was also put to death. It is said that he was in contact with Demosthenes and incited rebellion. Alexander asked his father's great general, Parmenion, to do the deed. Amyntas, son of Perdicaas, was accused of plotting against Alexander and executed. He had been the rightful heir to the Macedonian throne when Philip seized power and Philip married him to his daughter, Cynnane. His friend, also called Amyntas, but son of Antiochus, fled to Egypt for fear of being accused of plotting against the king.

Swiftly the young king acted to secure his borders, riding, as always, his fiery horse, Bucephalus. This horse was reputed to have been a present to Philip, but when taken out to a field for inspection, proved impossible to break in. However, the twelve year old Alexander, although his father had ordered the removal of the horse, thought he could master the animal. And so he did, to the applause of all watching. Philip presented him with Bucephalus and Alexander was the only person able to ride the spirited stallion. He even taught it to kneel later so that, when in armour, it was easier for him to mount.

Alexander put down an insurrection in Thessaly. When the Thessalanians would not let him pass through the Vale of Tempe, we see signs of his determination and inventiveness for the first time. He cut steps into the rocky sides of the nearby steep Mount Ossa to allow his troops through, suprising the enemy by attacking from their rear. He set out for the Danube, where his father had been wounded in the thigh some months before by a tribe called the Triballians. Alexander had been with him and now was the time to take his revenge. When faced with the problem of crossing the Danube, Alexander ordered his troops to fill their tents, which were made of leather, with straw and sew them together to make rafts. No Macedonian had ever heard of this, but Alexander had read Xenophon, who had described this method of crossing the Euphrates when he led his Ten Thousand Greeks back to their homeland, all those years before. We will hear of Alexander using the same method again.

Perhaps around this time Alexander ordered the completion of a circular building in the sanctuary at Olympia. It had been begun by his father, Philip, after the battle of Chaeronea and its ruins can be seen today. It housed gold and ivory statues of Philip, his wife, his parents and Alexander.

The young king moved against the Illyrians and rumour reached Thebes that he was dead, for when, urged on by Demosthenes and with the aid of Persian money, Thebes rebelled and tried to expel the Macedonian garrison, Alexander was nowhere to be seen. But the goddess Demeter warned the people of their coming destruction. And there were bad omens. Before the Battle of Leuktra, when Epaminondas won the day, spiders had spun white webs over the doors of Demeter's sanctuary. Now their silken threads were black.

The Macedonian army, led by Alexander's great friend and commander, Perdicaas, attacked Thebes and suddenly, almost magically, Alexander appeared outside the city walls. Magically, for Thebes is set in a great, flat plain and it is difficult to see how Alexander approached without being seen. However, his arrival was certainly magical in another sense, for he had marched his army, from Illyria, more than three hundred miles in two weeks, through difficult and mountainous terrain.

Thebes, the city that had once allied itself with the Persian king, Xerxes, was razed to the ground, only the house of Pindar the poet left standing. The king admired the poet, who had once sung the praises of Alexander I at the Olympic Games.

Alexander was twenty one years old. He had proved himself

in battle and shown a streak of ruthlessness. He had visited the oracle at Delphi and been told that he was invincible. His generals, war seasoned and battle hardened, were prepared to follow the commands of this charismatic young soldier king who now looked towards Persia. He would finish what his father had begun and defeat Greece's greatest enemy, Darius III, King of the Persians, who ruled his vast empire from his palace at Persepolis, the ruins of which can be seen today, situated about 40 miles north east of Shiraz, in Iran. Alexander had to borrow money to equip and supply his Macedonian army of about twenty thousand men, but Greece helped out with five thousand mercenaries and about seven thousand allied troops. Leaving Antipater to govern Macedonia with about thirteen thousand men, he marched for the Hellespont, or the Dardanelles as we know them today.

It was spring, 334 BC. We must try and imagine this army on the march. Five thousand cavalry certainly meant at least ten thousand horses, for each of the King's Companions had his slave, also mounted. Rations for these horses, over thirty thousand men and the pack animals, had to be carried. Tents, clothing and weapons had to be transported. Seige machines were bulky, but to save carriage, many of the parts of these machines were made in place, cut from local wood. This army marched from Pella, in Macedonia, to the Hellespont, by a coastal route, the fleet keeping in contact with them all the way.

The three hundred and fifty miles took twenty days.

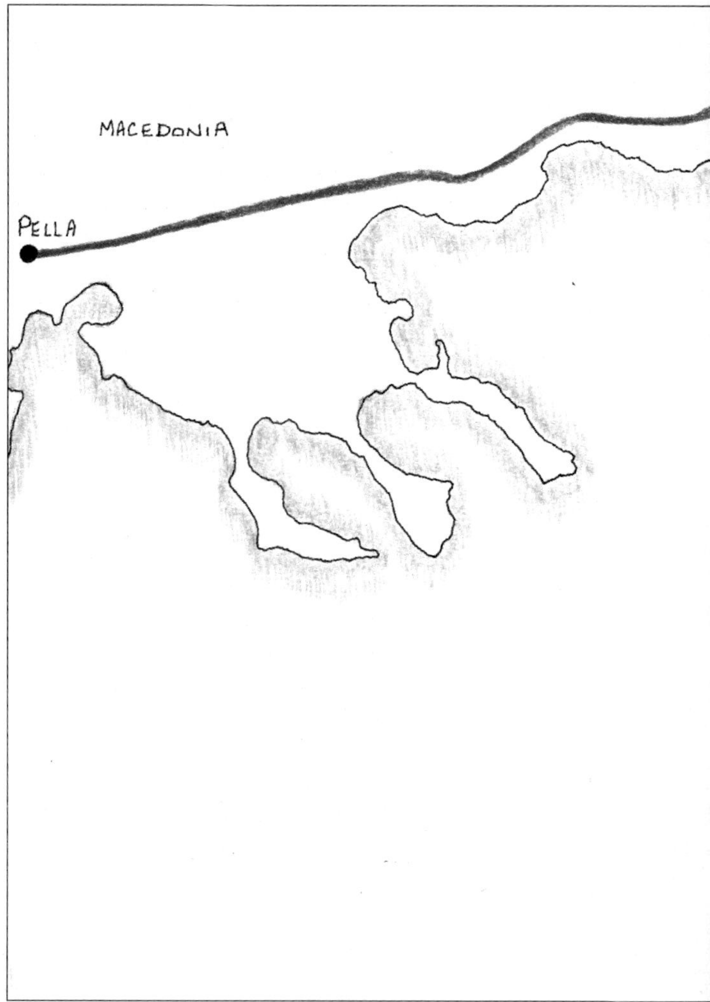

Map 2

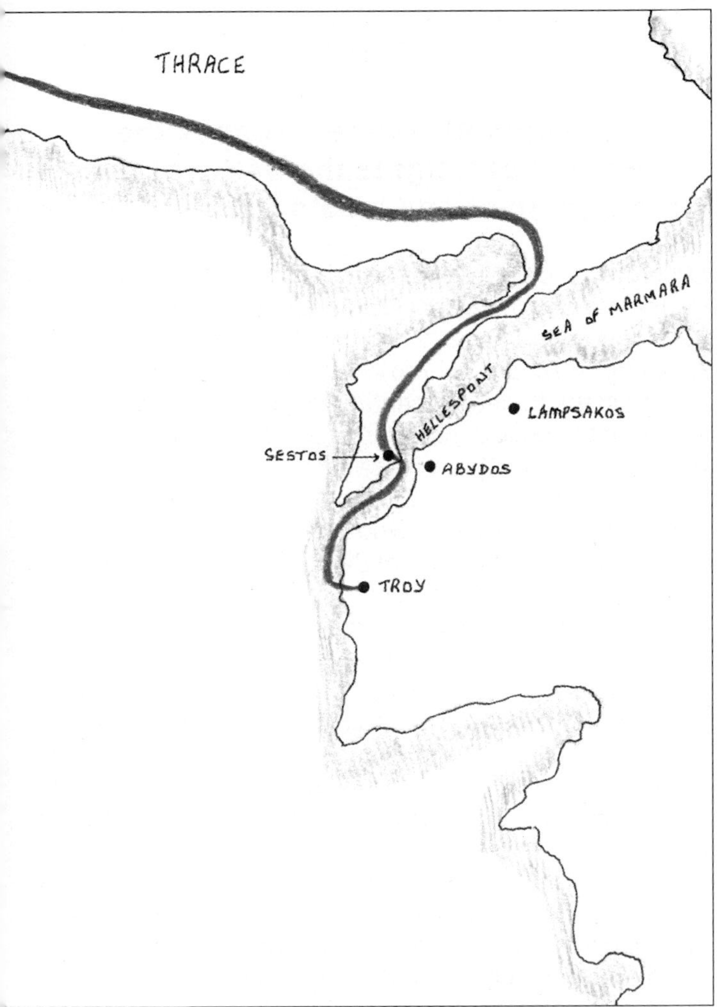

Alexander's journey from Pella to Troy -334 BC

Part 3

In which Alexander crosses the Hellespont, fights the Battle of the Granicus River and meets Darius at Issus.

Ordering his general, Parmenion, to take the army across the Hellespont to Abydos, Alexander took some of his small fleet and sailed around the coast to the harbour of the Achaens, the nearest shore to Troy. Here Agamemnon had landed in the thirteenth century BC, to begin the long war with the city whose prince, Paris, had abducted the beautiful Helen. Alexander threw his spear into the soil and claimed Persia as his. In Troy we are told that he sacrificed at the tomb of Achilles, his hero, who had been mortally wounded by an arrow from the bow of Paris. It had struck him in his only vulnerable part, his heel.

Before Schliemann uncovered the ruins of Troy andMycenae, the work of Homer was seen as purely mythical. However, in recent times the shadowy figures of Agamemnon and those who took part in the Trojan War have become clearer. If Alexander's historians reported that he visited Achilles' tomb, who are we, now, to disbelieve? It is said that Hephaestion sacrificed at the tomb of Achilles' dearest friend, Patroclus.

Before leaving Troy, Alexander visited the temple to Athena where a statue of a Persian governor of the region lay fallen. Learning from his seers that it was a good omen, he made sacrifice to the goddess, dedicating his armour to her, taking the most dazzling suits of armour from the temple for himself. It is said he wore the best when he first faced the enemy.

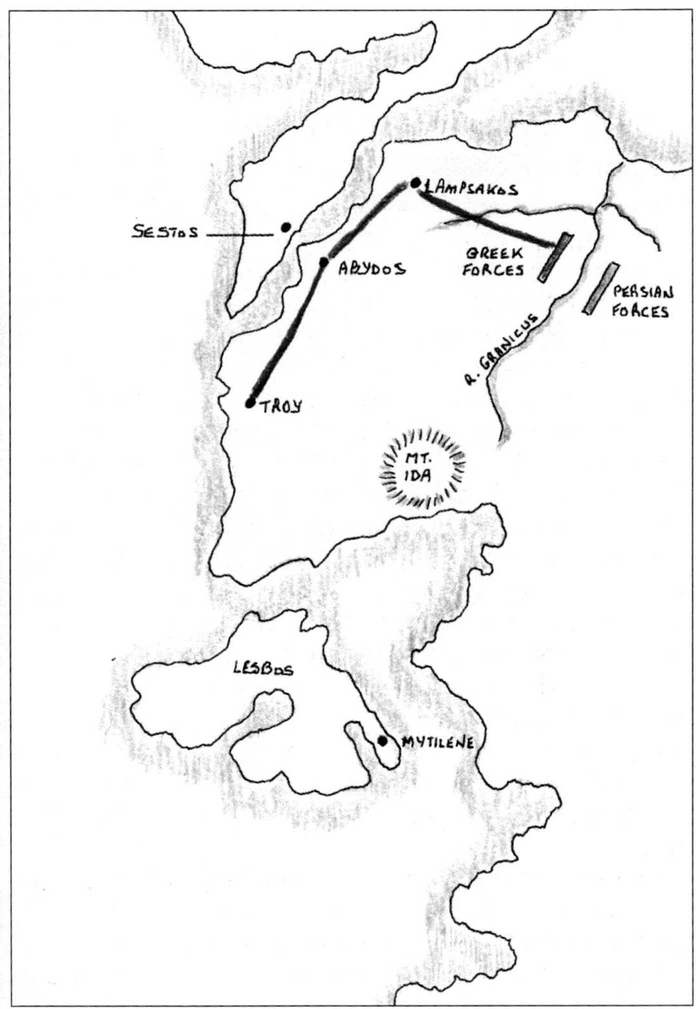

Map 3   *Alexander's journey from Troy to the Granicus river 334 BC.*

Battle at Granicus.

All Greeks of the time believed firmly in the gods of Olympus and the messages received from them through signs, omens and oracles. Joined by his army, Alexander reviewed his troops. 12,000 of the infantry were his own highly trained Macedonians, 7,000 were allies and 5,000 were mercenaries. There were archers, scouts, Shield Bearers and 4,500 cavalry, almost half of which latter were Macedonian. The King's Companions were commanded by Parmenion's son, Philotas, another friend of Alexander. With Alexander, always, went his young, slow witted half brother, Arrhidaeus.

Alexander led his army along the coast, through Lampsakos, towards the Granicus river where the Persians lay waiting. Pausanias, the Greek writer who travelled all over Greece in the 2nd century AD, tells a story about Lampsakos, a

3.

city on the Hellespont which had always sided with Persia. Alexander threatened the citadel with dire punishment and the people sent a man who had once been Alexander's teacher, to plead with him. Alexander, who knew why Anaximenes was coming to see him, swore by the gods that he would do the opposite of whatever he asked. Anximenes, however, must have known the king very well, for, so the story goes, he begged Alexander to take the women and children of Lampsakos into slavery, raze the city and its temples. Alexander, thwarted, pardoned Lampsacos and its people.

It was courage that won the young king his first battle. The Persian army, not led by Darius who was biding his time, was somewhat smaller than Alexander's (the historians who reported that they outnumbered the Macedonians three to one perhaps believed in the divinity of Alexander) had gathered on the far side of the Granicus river.

Alexander ignored the advice of his general, Parmenion, not to cross the water. His men had traversed the Hellespont, and the Granicus was nothing in comparison. He charged the enemy, who were led by Memnon, a mercenary from Rhodes and the battle was won due to the courage of the cavalry and Alexander, who fought in their midst and suffered a head wound which was, luckily, not serious. Turning to face his attacker, he did not see a sword descending and Cleitus, commander of a squadron of the royal cavalry, saved his life. Some say there were around 12,000 Persian dead and 20,000 taken captive. Alexander lost 129 men, most of them the king's Companions. Memnon escaped.

The historian, Arrian, tells us that Alexander visited his wounded, comforting them, inviting each of them to tell how they received their injuries and encouraging them to boast of their bravery in battle. He buried the Persian dead. He buried his own Companions in full armour with honour, commissioning his sculptor, Lysippus, to cast statues of them in bronze. Their relatives were excused all taxes. Those Greek prisoners, who had fought against him in Memnon's army, he had bound and sent to Macedonia to a life of hard labour.

Alexander's sculptor, Lysippus, was from Sikyon. The poet Archelaus wrote, of a statue of Alexander, "Lysippus formed in brass the courage high of Alexander and his aspect bold:
The brass looks up to heaven and seems to cry:
The earth is mine: thou, Jove, Olympus hold".

Alexander marched to Sardis, whose commander (news of Memnon's defeat must have spread quickly), surrendered the city and its treasury to him. These valuables served to fund the needs of the army. Continuing on his way, Alexander founded the new city of Smyrna after a dream. He was out hunting on Mount Pagos when he came across a holy place dedicated to Nemesis, divine vengeance. To the front of the sanctuary flowed a spring, shaded by a plane tree. Sitting in the shade of the tree, Alexander fell asleep and Nemesis appeared to him in his dream, commanding him to build a city there and populate it with the people of Smyrna. Pausanias tells us that the Smyrnians asked the advice of an oracle and were told that they would be happier and live longer, on Mount Pagos. So they moved.

Alexander journeyed on to Ephesus, a Greek city where his father's advance forces had once expelled the Persian military command which had, after some months, returned. Now Alexander once more banished the Persians and the people joyously went on the rampage, stoning the families of their occupiers. Alexander put a stop to this, forbidding all acts of revenge.

Still in Ephesus, Alexander ordered the rebuilding of the temple to Artemis, goddess of hunting, requesting it to be dedicated in his name. His request was refused, for the people said that one god should not honour another. And he was worshipped as divine for centuries after in that city, where temples were built and games organised in his honour.

Alexander marched for Miletus. The city lay on a headland and its governor, knowing that the Persian navy was not far away, refused to surrender. Alexander moved quickly, taking the outer city with ease and blocking the harbour with his fleet. When the Persian ships arrived, they far outnumbered his own and Parmenion, so the story goes, advised him to fight, for he had seen an omen, an eagle, sitting on the beach, near the Greek fleet.

Alexander, if the tale is true, for the second time did not take his general's advice. Although he believed firmly in omens, he interpreted this one in a different way. Because the eagle sat on the land, he said, his victory would be a land one. His strength lay in his seige equipment and soon the inner city fell to him. The Persian fleet, lying off shore, was

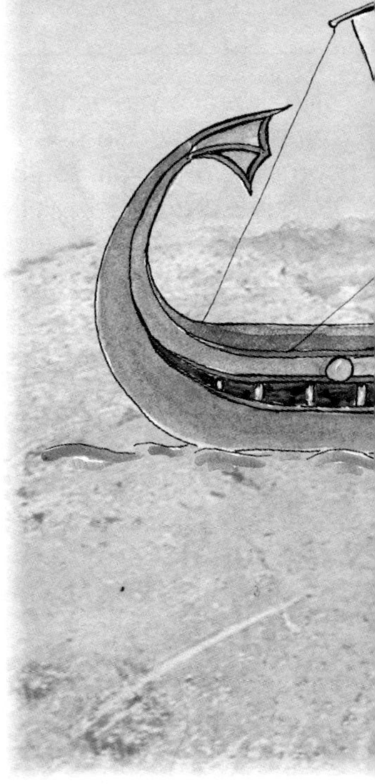

4.

An eagle sitting on a beach.

unable to obtain provisions or fresh water and had to sail away.

Alexander sold the soldiers who had not escaped into slavery but spared the private citizens. Wherever Alexander went, he left in place those governors who pledged allegiance to him and garrisoned the city with Macedonian troops. To those citzens who surrendered and recognised his sovereignty, he was lenient. But to those who rose against him, there was no mercy.

At this point, Alexander decided he could do without his navy and sent the main fleet home. It is possible that this was a clever move to prevent any of his men leaving, but it is also possible that, rather than attack Persia's powerful navy, Alexander chose, after his recent experience, to conquer the land bases which supplied the Persian fleet. But first he had Memnon to worry about. The Persian commander had retreated to Halicarnassus, a city situated in the area of Caria, sending his wife, Barsine and his son to the Persian King Darius, for safety. This is the same Barsine, daughter of the exiled Persian Artabazus, who had fled to Philip's court when Alexander was a boy.

A little distance from Halicarnassus, Alexander was hailed by a woman, Ada, once Queen of Caria. She begged for help. In her family, women ruled by tradition but she had reached middle age a childless widow. Her brother, Pixodarus, had banished her and taken over as governor. Pixodarus had once gone to Philip's court to propose marriage between his daughter and Alexander's slow witted half brother, Arrhidaeus. The nineteen year old Alexander had seen this as a threat to his inheritance. He thought that he should be the one to marry the girl. Philip, who had been hoping that a tie with Caria would be useful before he invaded Persia, but wanted something better for Alexander, lost his temper with the boy and Pixodarus took fright and left. His daughter married an Iranian. It was this Iranian who, on the death of Pixodarus, now ruled Caria.

Alexander supported Ada's claim to the throne and Ada is reputed to have adopted him as her son. One way or another, the local people were won over and Alexander continued towards Halicarnassus.

This was a city with strong fortifications and here Alexander suffered several setbacks. The great stone walls of the metropolis were protected by a wide, deep ditch. This had to be filled in before the siege towers could be placed in position.

But once in place, the wooden siege machines were burned by the opposition. The citizens defended their city for two long, hot summer months. One of Alexander's veteran soldiers, Atarrhias, distinguished himself when younger men were hesitating, turning the tide of battle against the Persians and Memnon and his men eventually fled to the island of Cos. Ada was restored to her throne and given Macedonian troops to help her keep control.

Before going any further, Alexander made the popular decision to send home all his Macedonian soldiers who had been married before they left. It was autumn, and he sent his general, Parmenion, back to Sardis with the cavalry, some foreign troops and the supply wagons, with orders to winter there and rejoin him in the Spring.

Mytilene surrendered, as did the island of Rhodes. In Corinth, at the Isthmian Games, the Greek people voted to send ambassadors to Alexander, bearing a golden crown, an honour they at last felt due to him.

Alexander took the rest of his army and turned south and then east, subduing the coastal lands as he progressed through Lycia and Pamphylia. His loyal troops must have suffered much privation during the coldest months of the year on the rugged, mountainous south coast of what we know now as Turkey. At about this time, a letter was intercepted by Parmenion, from the Persian king, Darius, to Alexander Lyncestes who was wintering in Sardis with the general. It spoke of gold and a plot to kill Alexander. Parmenion sent a messenger to inform Alexander, who sent the man back with orders for the arrest of Lyncestes.

It was spring at last when Alexander and his army turned towards the north from Phaselis, where they had wintered, to meet up with Parmenion. First, he marched his army along a narrow beach at the foot of Mount Climax, a beach which was, as a rule, under water. However, when the north wind blew, the waters receded for a few hours, exposing the thin strip of sand. With Lady Luck on his side, Alexander began his march, the north wind blew strongly and his army crossed the beach. When the men looked back at where they had been, the beach was no longer to be seen. The legend grew that Alexander, like the Dane who once ruled England as King Canute, could command the waves!

On reaching Gordium Alexander awaited the arrival of the general, the rest of the army and re-inforcements which had been sent for. But it was almost into summer when 4,000 Macedonian, Greek and allied forces arrived.

News was received of Memnon's activities. He had taken the islands of Chios and Lesbos and he was busy stirring things up in Greece, sending monies to foster insurrection. Possibly Alexander also heard of his death, which was a stroke of luck for the young king. Certainly Darius, King of Persia, heard and was dismayed at losing a man of his experience.

Before leaving the city, Alexander cut the famous knot of Gordius. And here Lady Luck appeared again, for the cutting was accompanied by a dramatic thunder storm, signifying to his men the approval of Zeus, the god of gods.

Summer, 333 BC, exactly three years after becoming king, found Alexander not far from the Cilician Gates, a narrow and reputably impregnable hill pass. The governor of Cilicia fled, ordering the land around to be burned, in the hopes of depriving the Macedonian army of food and provision.

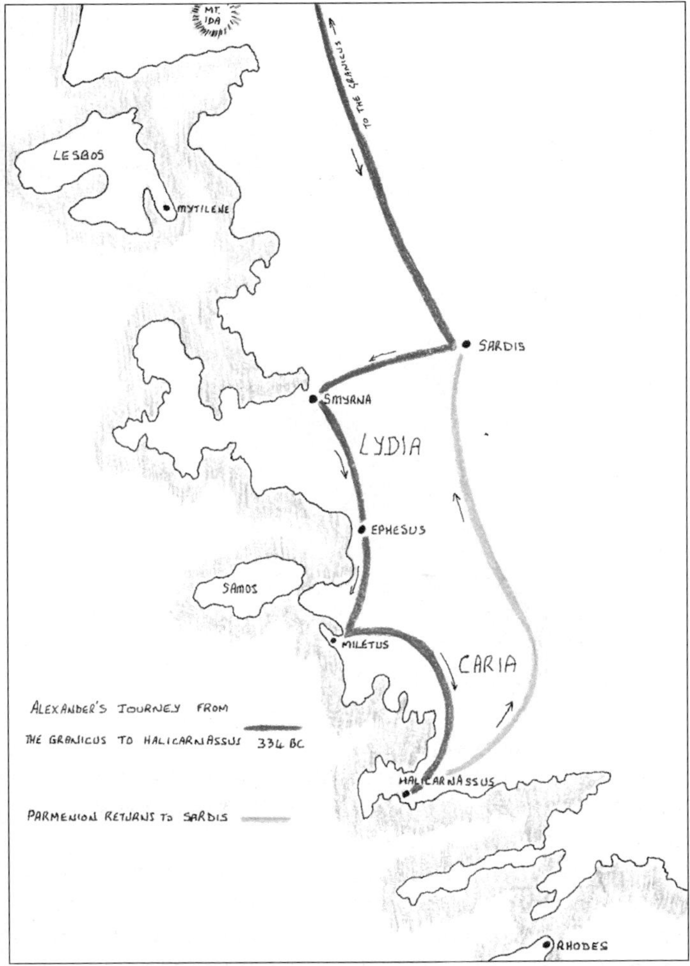

Map 4 — Alexander's journey from the Granicus to Halicarnassus 334 BC. — Parmenion returns to Sardis.

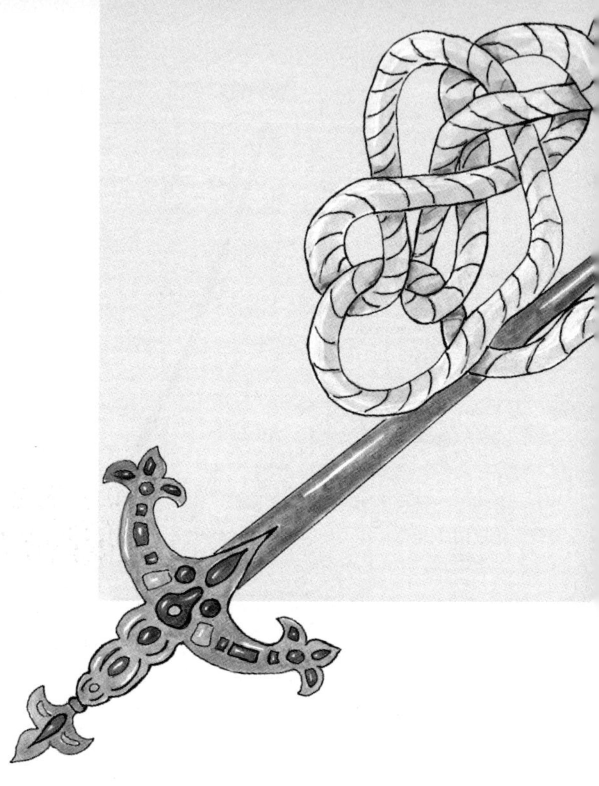

The Gordium knot is cut.

He left a small contingent at the pass, no match for the fast and lightly armed units of archers and cavalry that Alexander himself led through. The burning was stopped and Alexander hurried on to Tarsus.

Summer, and a dusty, hot and sweaty king plunged into the river Cydnus for relief. But the waters of the river flowed cold from the surrounding snowy mountains and Alexander caught a chill. He lay ill for some time and the story goes that he was having difficulty with his breathing and was expected to die, when Philip, a Greek who had been a

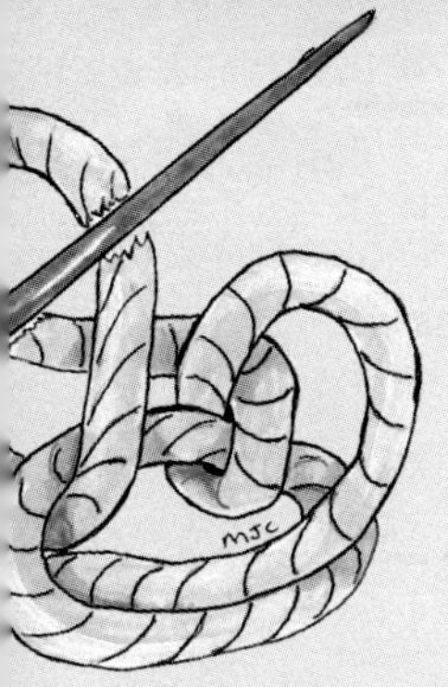

companion to the child Alexander at Philip's court and had some medical knowledge, offered to treat him. Alexander agreed, but received a letter from Parmenion, stating that Philip had been bribed by Darius to poison him. Alexander ignored the letter, drank the potion mixed by Philip, recovered and celebrated his return to health. He sacrificed to the gods and organised athletic events, a race held by torch light and literary competitions. But he had been ill for many weeks and Darius had time to go to Babylon and muster his forces. From Babylon, Darius marched towards Issus. Alexander marched quicker and got there before him, left his sick and wounded there and turned south to meet his arch enemy, the Persian king. The two armies passed during the night, perhaps within miles of each other, each unaware of the other's presence, difficult to believe in these days of instant communication.

Darius reached Issus and found Alexander's field hospital where he cut off the hands of the sick. A cruel and senseless act which did him no good, for some escaped, reached Alexander and warned him that Darius was now behind him.

BLACK SEA
SEA OF MARMARA
GRANICUS BATTLE
TROY
LESBOS
CHIOS
SAMOS
SARDIS
EPHESUS
CARIA
HALICARNASSUS
RHODES
PHASELIS

Map 5

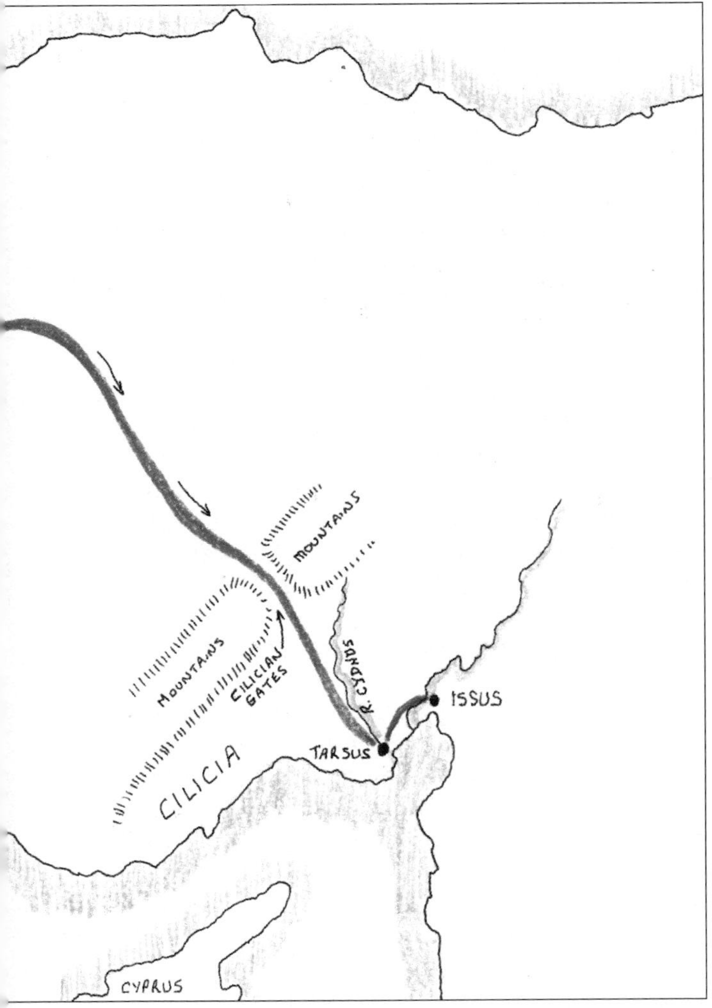

Alexander's journey from Halicarnassus to Issus 333 BC.

And so the two great armies met at Issus, on the muddy banks of a river. It is said that Darius, when reviewing his troops before the battle, had asked the opinion of Charidemus, the Athenian general who had joined him when exiled from Athens by Alexander. Charidemus, seeing Darius' magnificently clad army, resplendent in rich colours, chariots shining with gold, replied honestly that the sight of the army could strike terror into anyone's heart, yet although the Macedonian troops were rougher, they were also tougher. They did not live in luxury. The earth was their bed at night, and they found food where they could. They were disciplined to the last man, fighting as one unit. Charidemus suggested that Darius hire Hellenes, then he would have real soldiers. As can be expected, he was put to death.

Alexander also reviewed his troops. He visited each unit, recalling their brave deeds, addressing many of his men by name. He reminded them that the gods were on their side. He reminded the Greek contingents of the way Xerxes, the Persian king, had ill treated them, and to those who lived by pillaging, he pointed out the riches to be had if they won the battle.

For once, the great Macedonian Phalanx was at a disadvantage in the muddy conditions. Although outnumbered, Alexander won the day through his courage in leading the cavalry, the brave King's Companions, into the thick of battle. At one time, he came close to Darius' chariot, but the Persian king was protected by his brother, Oxathres, who fought fiercely and Darius leapt from his chariot on to a waiting horse and fled, throwing away his royal robe and shield, which could identify him, as he went. A mosaic, found in the House of the Faun at Pompeii, dating from the 2nd century BC, depicts the moment of their meeting in colour and dramatic detail. Alexander pursued Darius well into the night, but in vain. When he returned to the Persian camp, deserted by the enemy, the only thing left that had not been plundered by his men was the tent of Darius. He bathed a wound in his thigh and washed away the stains of battle in a magnificent bath, surrounded by the opulence of Persian royalty, gold, silver, rich jewels and everywhere the smell of incense. "So this", he remarked, "is what it means to be King".

The next morning Alexander, accompanied by Hephaestion and having visited his wounded in spite of his own injury, went to see some of the captives. These were Darius' mother, Sisgambis and his beautiful wife, Statira, who was accompanied by her children. He had heard them weeping the previous evening, for they thought Darius was dead and he had sent someone to reassure them. Now the Queen Mother, Sisigambis, bowed deeply to Hephaestion, who was taller and so more striking than Alexander. Embarassed on discovering her mistake, she was put at ease by Alexander, who said that she had not made a mistake. His friend, too, was an Alexander.

The Queen was allowed to bury any Persian dead. She, her children and her motherin-law were allowed to keep their royal status and given their own quarters. Their possessions were returned to them and all the time they were in captivity they enjoyed royal protection.

Parmenion was sent to Damascus to sieze the royal treasure. The 2,600 talents worth of coins surrendered to him provided all back pay and would keep the army for another six months. There were another 500 talents of silver and some pack animals,which were used to ferry the treasure back to Alexander, along with Per- sian wives and children. Amongst the women was Barsine, wife of Memnon, who had been sent to Darius for safety, from Halicarnassus. Alexander took her as his mistress. Alexander also took possession of a lovely golden casket into which he placed his precious copy of the Iliad. It is said that Darius wrote to Alexander, asking for the return of his family and that Alexander replied that they were there whenever he wished to collect them.

Alexander now turned south, to take the cities on the Mediterranean coast and so prevent, as planned, the Persian navy from provisioning and manning its fleet. Sidon surrendered to him and, as it had once been a monarchy, Hephaestion was asked to choose a king. This was not an easy task, as at once he was surrounded by eager citizens, greedy for the position. The story goes and perhaps it is a legend, that Hephaestion was staying in the house of a noble subject and offered the throne to him. But it was refused, for

6.

Darius at Issus.

the young man protested that the throne had to be given to one of royal blood. He knew one such man, but he was a poor gardener, named Abdalonymus, who was astonished when Hephaestion and his host arrived and presented him with the royal robes of office. Alexander was said to be struck by his honesty and noble bearing and presented him with a large portion of Persian booty.

In the January of 332 BC, Alexander attacked Tyre, a walled city that had, three hundred years previously, withstood a thirteen year long siege by Nebuchadnezzar, the Mesopotamian king who had built the Hanging Gardens of Babylon. Tyre stood on an island, half a mile out at sea and it had its own fleet of ships. Alexander decided to build a breakwater out to the island. As the mole grew in length, the builders came within reach of Tyre's fleet as well as the defences on the city walls and had to deal with fire ships and bombardment. The breakwater cracked and was washed away. Alexander, not to be deterred, began another mole, wider and stronger than the first, and he placed two towers at the end of it, manned with soldiers, to defend the work. Alexander set out for Sidon to obtain ships. He returned with a fleet of two hundred but the harbour was closed to him. When he broke through and approached the city walls, his ships were bombarded with red hot sand and his men threw themselves into the sea in agony. The young king mounted great stonethrowing catapults and portable siege towers on his ships. He positioned himself on the highest tower and at last the walls of the city were breached, six months after the beginning of the siege. A pardon was announced for all who sought refuge in the temples. Some citizens complied but thousands were killed or taken in slavery. Darius wrote again, offering peace in return for his family.

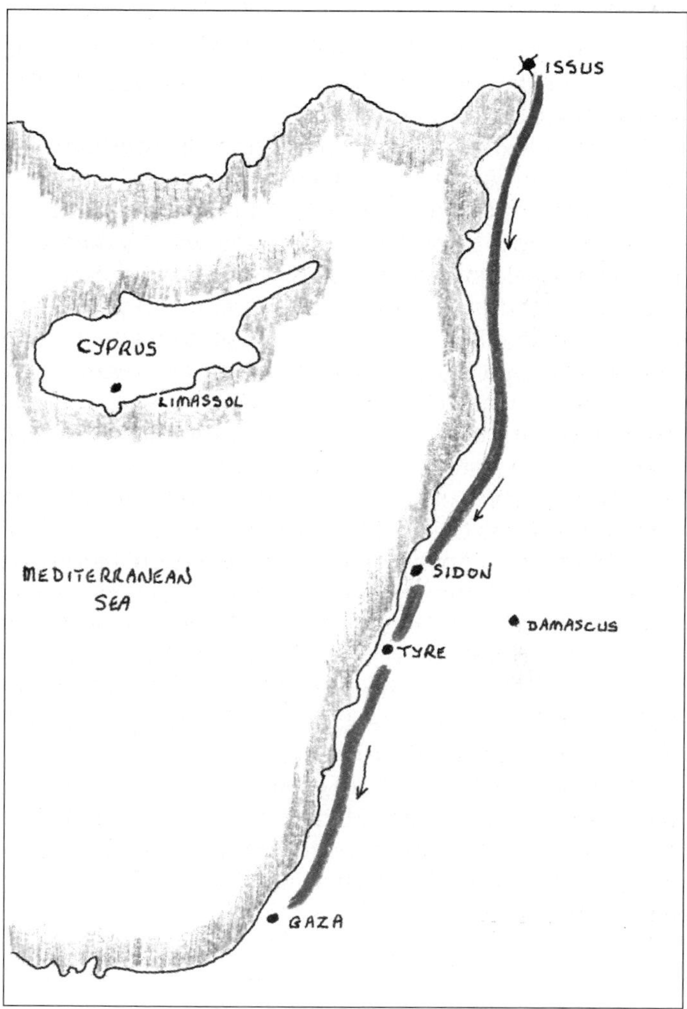

Map 6   *From Issus to Gaza 333-332 BC.*

Parmenion is reputed to have advised,"If I were you, I would accept." Alexander's reply, so the story goes, was, "If I were you, I would, but I am Alexander."

Gaza was Alexander's next challenge. It stood on a hill and he was advised that it was too high for his siege towers. Never one to back down from a challenge, Alexander ordered a great mound to be built below the walls, which would raise the height of his towers and, at the same time, ordered his engineers to burrow under the walls. It was summer in Gaza and it says something for the force of Alexander's personality that a war weary army toiled in the heat and, after two months, broke through the city"s defences. Alexander, as usual in the forefront of battle, was wounded in the shoulder by a bolt from an enemy catapult. The bolt was extracted, leaving a deep wound which bled so much that, although he plunged straight back into the fray, Alexander fainted.

Gaza fell and the governor, Betis, was brought before the king, refusing to kneel before him. Alexander had him tied to the back of his chariot and dragged around the city as Achilles had dragged Hector around Troy. Persian losses had been great, but so had Macedonian, and Alexander sent home for reinforcements before setting out for Egypt. He also sent to Macedon, to one of his old tutors, Leonidas, a man who had been not only severe but also somewhat parsimonious, a richness of frankincense. Léonidas had once prevented the young prince from throwing incense on to a sacrificial fire, saying that he must be careful with such an expensive item.

Part 4

Alexander enters Egypt, becomes Pharaoh and visits an Oracle.

Six days' march brought Alexander to Pelusium at the head of the Nile Delta. When an army the size of Alexander's marched, the head of the column was a very long way from the rear. Alexnader would send his dispatch runner back and forth along the line with messages. His name was Philonides, he must have been a tireless runner, who was also used for measuring road stages. A statue was erected in his honour at Olympia, in the south west corner of the Altis and Pausanias, the Greek traveller, mentions seeing it in the 2nd century AD.

Hephaestion was waiting to meet Alexander at Pelusium, with his remaining ships. He had on board pirates and others taken prisoner in the Aegean and despots who had been removed from Lesbos, Cos and Chios. The pirates were put to death and the others punished as Alexander saw fit. Egypt had not been happy under Persian rule and the local governor or "Satrap" met Alexander with enthusiasm, offering gold and all his furniture in return for his safety. The Macedonians sailed up the Nile and Alexander marched by land to meet them in Memphis. We can only imagine what Alexander and his army felt as they gazed on the vast, smooth, limestone covered Pyramids and the enigmatic Sphinx. Those monuments must have been in pristine condition in his time. The ancient city of Memphis is reputed to have been magnificent, covering an area of over five square miles and its governor ruled from the "Palace of the White Walls".

Here Alexander was made Pharaoh and he sacrificed to the Egyptian bull god Apis. The tombs of these bulls were at nearby Saqqarah. The festivities which followed his crowning included athletic and artistic competitions.

Sailing back down the Nile to its mouth, Alexander arrived at Lake Mareotis. There he paced out the land from the lake to the sea and ordered the building of a city, to be called Alexandria. Lacking something to mark the boundaries of the area, he used grain. When the birds came and ate it, it was regarded by his seers as a good omen, signifying a prosperous city. For 600 years it was one of the major cities of ancient times and held one of the world's greatest libraries, founded by Alexander's friend and historian, Ptolemy, who ruled Egypt after Alexander's death. The first lighthouse was built there in 270 BC, of white marble and was one of the Seven Ancient Wonders of the World.

From Lake Mareotis, Alexander set out with a small party, into the desert, for Siwa - today an oasis town lying on an ancient caravan route in Egypt's Western Desert, about 293 miles south west of Alexandria. In Alexander's time it was the place of the oracle of the Egyptian god Ammon, often known as the Sun god, Ammon-Ra. The Greeks identified Ammon with Zeus, calling him Zeus-Ammon and Perseus and Heracles were said to have visited his temple at Siwa. Alexander claimed Heracles as his ancestor and perhaps it was for this reason that he expressed a wish to visit the oasis. The oracle would have been well known to the king. The poet Pindar, much admired by Alexander, had written a poem to Zeus-Ammon and had set up a statue to him in his home city of Thebes. Athens had once sent a gift of gold to Siwa and there was a temple dedicated to the god in Piraeus.

7.

The Egyptian god, Ammon.

Some say that Alexander had never been sure of his parentage (his mother had once hinted that Philip was not his father) and the journey into the desert was undertaken to learn something of himself. He had been made a Pharaoh and Pharaohs were worshipped by the Egyptians as sons of Ammon. Certainly after his visit, coins were struck bearing his head wearing thecurling ram's horn, emblem of the god.

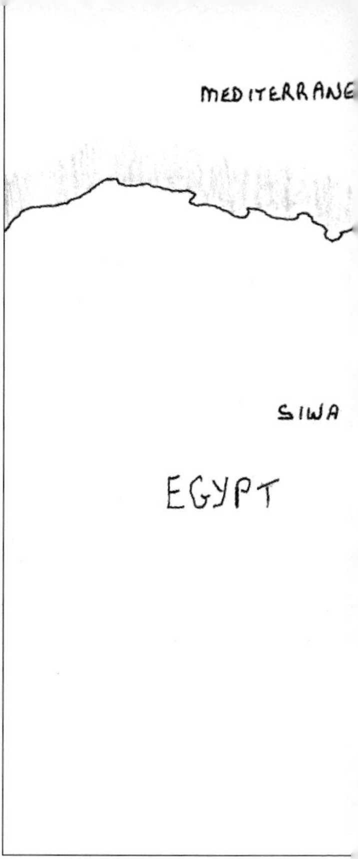

It was not a journey to be taken lightly across undulating dunes and Alexander and his party suffered from the burning heat. They lost their way in a sand storm, wandering around for some days and ran out of water. Here Tyche, or Lady Luck played her part, for a sudden rain storm occurred, so fierce that the men were able to quench their thirst and fill their containers. Alexander's companions must have thought the gods were watching over them and so were ready for the pronouncement of the priests at Siwa. They reached a range of hills and the way grew rugged. They marched in the coolness of the night, the moonlight shining eerily on

Map 7

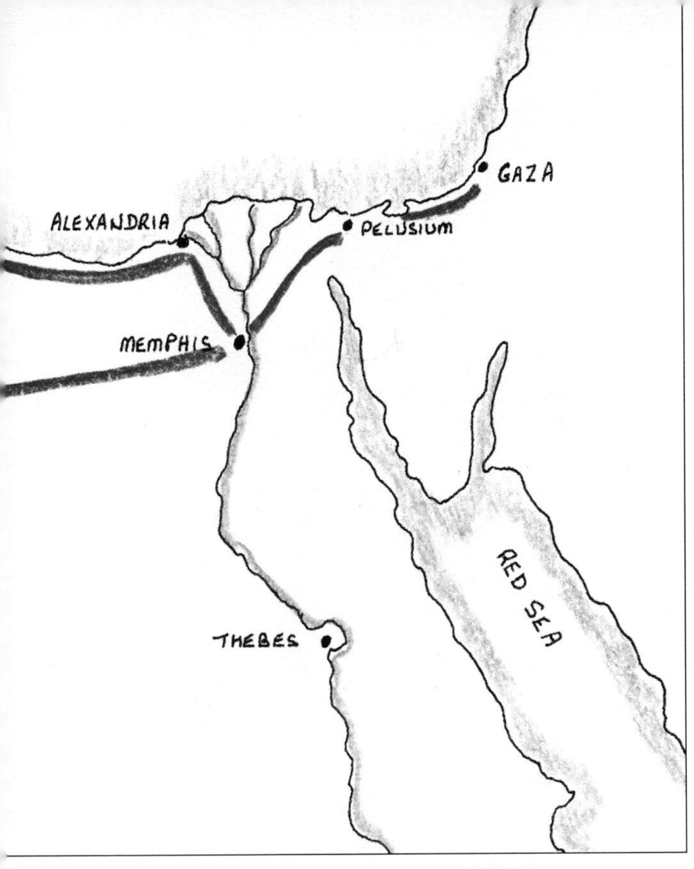

Alexander in Egypt - 332 BC.

the bleached shells which lay on the ground and embedded in the rocks around them.

After many days in the desert they were led by some crows, although some say by hissing snakes, to the site of the oracle, an area so thick with trees that the sun could barely penetrate. Fresh water springs abounded, wrote one historian and there was one spring which was warm in the morning, cool

8.   *Alexander makes an offering to Amon.*

in the heat of the midday sun, warmer in the evening and boiling hot at night.

When Alexander approached the oracle, he was met by priests who hailed him as the divine son of Zeus. The questions he asked of the god, along with the answers, were never disclosed. His companions, though, asked the oracle if they should regard the king as divine and were told that Zeus would approve. Long after he was dead, even into the Christian era, Alexander was worshipped near Siwa along with Zeus-Ammon.

Back at Memphis, Alexander was feted as a god. He odered restoration work to begin on the temples destroyed or desecrated by the Persians in 343 BC. There is a lovely relief of Alexander carved in his honour on the outer walls of the temple at Luxor, depicting the king making an offering to Ammon.

Alexander sacrificed to Zeus and rested his army which had been reinforced by almost a thousand men sent from Antipater in Macedonia. They indulged in games and festivals.

Part 5

Alexander in Persia where he meets Darius once more.

Summer again. July 331 to be precise. Alexander was twenty five years old, the army getting restless and Darius, his great enemy, still had to be dealt with. Alexander departed Egypt, leaving governors, enough troops to garrison the land and a Greek, Cleomenes, who had been living in the Delta, to collect taxes. The army was marched towards the Euphrates river.

Darius, who had added terrible scythed chariots to his weaponry and increased his army to a quarter of a million men, marched again from Babylon, between the Tigris and Euphrates, adopting a scorched earth policy, sending his general, Mazaeus, with a few thousand men, to burn the area being approached by Alexander and so starve his army. But Alexander led his forces further north, where the weather was cooler and he had water and provisions. Hephaestion was sent ahead to build a bridge across the Euphrates, where Darius, anticipating the crossing, had commanded Mazaeus to prevent this. We do not know why Mazaeus did not carry out his orders, but he turned away and continued with the crop burning and Alexander carried on towards the Tigris.

In Persian the name Tigris means "arrow", an apt name for such a fast flowing river and it flowed most swift and strong at the point where Alexander had to cross. He split his cavalry in two, standing them in the water, which reached the horses necks, while the infantry crossed between them. Not a man was lost.

Alexander camped with the intention of resting his troops for two days, but on the night of the second, the 20th of September, a shadow gradually crept over the moon until at length its light was lost. Alexander, tutored by Aristotle, knew full well what an eclipse was, but to the terrified soldiers he said that it was a good omen. The darkened moon was Persia. They would eclipse her. They marched on, towards Darius.

As they advanced, news was brought to Alexander of the death of Darius' beautiful wife, who was still, with her mother-in-law and children, his captive. She had travelled with the army since the battle of Issus and the journey, with all its hardships, must have taken a toll of her health. The king rushed to her tent, wailing in grief. He ordered a one day fast and gave her a Persian funeral with full honours before continuing on his way, eventually pitching camp some miles from Guagamela, in whose plains lay Darius and his troops. When Alexander came to the hills overlooking Guagamela as dawn was breaking, hoping to take the Persians by surprise, a ripple of fear ran through his men. What a sight must have met their eyes as they looked down into the plain, a pall of dust adding an air of unreality to the scene, the early morning sun reflecting flashes of light from thousands of spears, helmets and chariots. What sounds must have filled their ears, the murmur of myriad voices and languages, the clank of armour and the restless neighing of horses. Alexander ordered his troops to lay down their arms and rest. He and some officers reconnoitered the ground before holding a council of war, when he was urged to attack that night, under cover of darkness. Alexander refused, saying he did not steal his victories. They would march the next morning. Was it this confident reply that restored moral to his frightened men? Or perhaps it was the fact that he retired to his tent that evening and slept so deeply that he had to be woken at dawn, when he rode out and exhorted his army as usual, praising them, greeting many of them by name again and recalling their individual deeds.

A bloody battle followed that September day on the plains of Guagamela. Darius' army

9.

outnumbered Alexander's by about six to one. His scythed chariots must have cut swathes through the enemy lines, cutting down horses and men alike. Confusion would have reigned, for after the long dry summer months, the dust thrown up would have been blinding and choking.

Alexander rode, as always, at the head of his cavalry. Historians agree that his speed, quick decisions and flexibility won him the battle. Darius fled and losses on both sides

Gifts of caged leopards.

must have been great. Alexander did not linger. In the seasonal heat the stench from the rotting corpses on the battlefield was noxious and the risk of disease great. He pushed thoughts of Darius from his mind for the time being and marched for Babylon. His route took him through the rich farm land between the Tigris and Euphrates, where the barley stood thick in the fields, date palms grew in abundance and his men could eat their fill.

The first to meet Alexander, while he was still some way from the city, was it's satrap or governor, Mazaeus. The same Mazaeus who had burned crops and been ordered to prevent Alexander from crossing the Euphrates. Had he anticipated the downfall of Darius? Was that why he disobeyed his orders? We will never know, but he surrendered himself, his family and his city to the young king.

Alexander approached the city with caution, but the gates in its great brick walls were thrown open, flowers were strewn in his path and the air was filled with the scent of incense. The city treasurer, Bagaphanes, welcomed him with gifts of caged leopards and lions and a procession of horse and cattle, followed by chanting priests and musicians.

The Persians had invaded Babylon in 539 BC, when Nebuchadnezzar's son, Belshazzar, was king. Belshazzar had given a great feast where the wine was abundant and suddenly a human hand appeared, writing on the palace wall. The frightened king called the prophet, Daniel, who was living in the court and asked him to interpret the words. We can read his answer in the Book of Daniel today:

"And this is the writing that is written, Mane, Mane, Tekel, Upharsin. This is the interpretation of the thing. Mane; God hath numbered thy kingdom and finished it. Tekel; Thou art weighed and found wanting. Peres; Thy kingdom is divided and given to the Medes and Persians." Daniel 5, 24-28.

"In that night was Belshazzar the king of the Chaldeans slain. And Darius the Mede took the kingdom, being about three score and two years old." Daniel 5, 30-31.

The people had not been happy under Persian rule. Xerxes had destroyed their temples and statues. Now Alexander had ousted another Darius. From the great riches of the royal treasury he gave the priests the money to restore their holy places. He paid his men handsome bonuses and relaxed in that wonderful city of flowing waters, gardens and the beautiful Gate of the love goddess, Ishtar. Parts of the city walls, which surrounded the city for twelve miles, were reputed to be four feet thick, coated in the bitumen which occurred naturally in a nearby lake. These walls, topped with towers, stood three hundred feet high and entrance was gained through a hundred brass gates.

Back in Greece, while Alexander had been busy in Asia, just before he defeated Darius at Arbela, Agis III of Sparta rebelled and Antipater, Alexander's viceroy, moved south with an army to defeat him at Megalopolis. Alexander is reputed to have been jealous of Antipater's success and referred to the battle as "a war of mice". He thought that he exceeded his powers and had his eye on the throne.

But in Babylon, Alexander and his men revelled, feasted and got drunk. The king, being well read, had no doubt heard of the Feast of Belshazzar and money was of no account. There was no hand to be seen but, figuratively speaking, the writing was on the wall. For after Susa, his next destination, there was a change in landscape, weather, people and perhaps in Alexander himself.

Mazaeus was left in place as governor of Babylon, given enough soldiers to garrison it and a Macedonian was presented with the post of treasurer. Alexander, travelling east, with one of his close friends, Harpalus, in charge of the wagons containing the valuables, was met by reinforcements from Greece, totalling about 15,000 men.

Three weeks after leaving Babylon Alexander entered Susa, accompanied by elephants and camels, gifts brought to him by the governor's son. He was said to be the first European ever to have elephants. Once in the city, Alexander found the treasure to be vast. There was gold bullion as well as silver, jewels, rich robes, silks and precious carpets. In the palace Alexander seated himself on Darius' throne. But the Persians were a tall race and among his own people Alexander was short. His feet could not reach the Persian king's footstool and a table had to be substituted. Alexander left Darius' mother and children in the palace, taking from it two statues which Xerxes had removed from Athens over 300 years before. These were returned to their rightful home. A glance at a relief map of the area will show how different the terrain was that Alexander had to travel on leaving Susa for the Persian frontier and the city of Persepolis. Expecting trouble from the local people, he split his army, ordering Parmenion to take the low route with the pack animals and heavy arms while he went into the mountains with the cavalry and light infantry.

After climbing for several days, Alexander and his party reached the pass, approached by a narrow canyon, known as the Persian Gates. Cautiously Alexander entered the gorge, to find his way blocked by a wall. Too late, he discovered the wall to be false.

Behind the wall and above the gorge the enemy lay in wait, to shower his men with rocks and boulders. Alexander, to his shame, had to retreat for the first time. Lady Luck had deserted him. He made camp about three miles away from the Gates and refused to take a route which skirted the gorge, for he could not leave his dead unburied. He divided his men. Some he left, to keep the fires burning and make the camp look busy. The rest he took, with a shepherd as a guide, on a high route that would bring them out behind the Persians' wall. Taking provisions for three days, Alexander led his group of lightly armed troops through rock, snow and dangerous drifts, very unfamiliar territory, until they gained the top. There, he again divided his men. Taking only a few, he suprised the foe by attacking from their rear and soon he was free to bury his dead, for the enemy had scattered. Linking up with the rest of his men, he was joined by Parmenion and the army ammounted to 60,000 men when he entered Persepolis, the city built by Darius I, the Persian king who had taken Babylon from Belshazzar. It was January of the year 330 BC.

At the top of the great staircase, at the Gate of Xerxes, the governor waited to greet the Alexander. In the palace treasury lay a richness of bullion greater than the king had ever seen. That and much of the already accumulated treasure had to be sent back to Athens. Thousands of pack animals were ordered for this and the effect of the arrival in Athens of these riches, about 360,000 talents (Athens had started the Peloponnesian War with 6,000 talents), together with the opening of the temple treasuries of Delphi, Athens and other sanctuaries which were secularised, was devastating. To add to the problem, the returning soldiers had been paid far more than local troops. Inflation was rampant, adversely affecting the city states and monumental arts.

Not all the treasure had been in the palace at Persepolis, however and Alexander allowed his troops, for the first time, to loot and pillage the rest of the city. As the soldiers ran amok, killing and destroying, eventually the king had to give orders for the women to be left alone. He held a banquet. A feast like that of Belshazzar, where the wine flowed free.

Women graced the hall in the great palace and musicians played. The revelry ended when the palace was burned to the ground.

When archaeologists disco- vered the remains of Perse- polis, they found three feet of ash in the Hall of Xerxes. Ptolemy said, in his writings, that Alexander set fire to the palace. Was it to avenge the sacking and burning of A- thens by the Persian Xerxes? Ptolemy says it was. Plutarch has another story. He bla- med it on the wine and a wo-

10.

man named Thais, who teased Alexander and was the first to throw a lighted torch, daring the king to follow suit. Certainly the wine flowed. But we learn that Thais was Ptolemy's mi- stress. No one knows the truth of the matter, only that Alexander regretted it, too late, for Persepolis burned.

Meanwhile, where was Darius? After the battle of Guagamela

lace was burned to the ground.

he had fled to Ecbatana, in Media, where Persians kings were wont to spend the summer months. It was a city surrounded by seven walls, each of a different colour, each one higher than the one in front, the last two plated in silver and gold.

At first Darius prepared to meet the Macedonian forces yet again, then changed his mind and left, with the intention of holding the pass in the mountains called the Caspian Gates. But there was treachery in his camp. Two of his own commanders, Bessus and Nabarzanes, plotted against him, eventually seizing him, binding him and throwing him in a cart, to trundle behind his own army.

Alexander led his men north out of Persepolis, there was nothing there to keep them, on the 450 mile long route to Ecbatana. There he received reinforcements in the shape of six thousand mercenaries, who had marched unchallenged from Greece. It was late spring of the year 330 BC. But Darius had already left when he arrived. Selecting a light and mobile force, Alexander moved fast towards the Caspian

Gates, found Darius' deserted camp and discovered that the Persian king's army had dispersed and Darius himself was in the hands of the traitor, Bessus. Alexander raced in pursuit of his greatest enemy and after two days' march reached a village where he was told that if he took a short cut through the desert, he could catch up with Bessus, who was travelling by night. Leaving behind his exhausted infantry, Alexander took five hundred of his best horses and raced on. At dawn the next day, ahead of his main body of men and accompanied by sixty Companions, Alexander came upon the enemy army and charged without hesitation. Many of the surprised Persians were unarmed and they scattered, very few offering resistance. But it was all in vain, for Alexander found Darius, fifty years old and the last of the great Achaemenid family, dead in a wagon, by the roadside, deserted by all. He is said to have wrapped him in his own cloak and, magnanimous as always, sent the body to Sisigambis, Darius' mother, to be buried with full royal honours. Nabarzanes was pardoned, perhaps because he presented Alexander with a beautiful young eunuch, Bargoas, with whom the king fell in love. Darius' brother, Oxathres, was made one of the King's Companions.

Alexander was King of Persia. The army had accumulated a vast ammount of treasure, Darius was dead and the troops must have thought that they would leave for home. But Alexander had other ideas. Perhaps he had been keyed up with the idea of finally meeting his arch enemy, only to find him dead. The adrenalin was still flowing. He had to do something more. His personal magnetism was surely great, for instead of mutinying, his men followed him on the next stage of his journey. After Bessus, killer of Darius.

Part 6

A plot uncovered, a friend killed and Alexander falls in love.

Parmenion was left in charge at Ecbatana, and Harpalus remained as guardian of the treasury. Later, when Alexander was on his way back from India, Harpalos absconded with a great deal of treasure, reached Crete by ship and was arrested in Athens. He bribed politician friends of Alexander and escaped. He fell in love with a prostitute and when she died he was able to build her a notable tomb, which Pausanias saw in the 2nd century AD, on the Sacred Way which ran from Athens to Eleusis, where the goddess Demeter was worshipped.

At about this time, Alexander had an idea which has been copied many times since. He ordered 30,000 young, hand picked Persian boys to be dressed in Macedonian dress and be trained, each in his own province, in Macedonian warfare.

Alexander travelled eastwards, along the coast of the Caspian Sea, through land green with trees, rich in rivers and wild flowers and many thought they were at the edge of the world where the Greeks had a river god, Oceanus, whose waters, they said, encircled the earth. One of the legends that abounded after Alexander's death suggests that the Queen of the Amazons approached Alexander at about this time and spent two weeks in his company, for she wanted to have his child. But what the king did do now, was to adopt Persian dress, about which we can imagine there was some murmuring. Persians had always been enemies of the

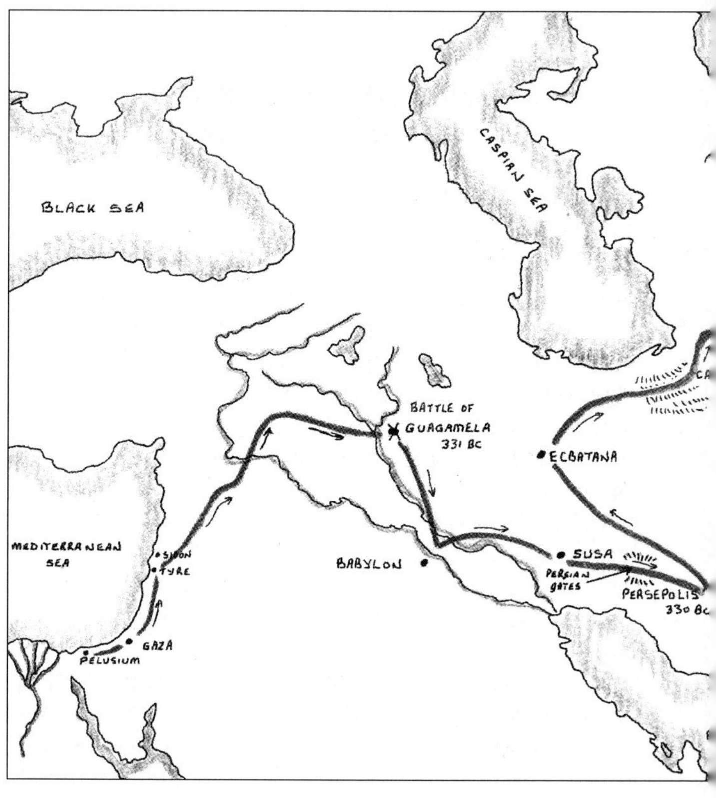

Map 8

Greeks and now they had one of them in the king's cavalry, one of them as the king's lover and the king himself was wearing a Persian royal diadem and tunic.

Four hundred miles from Ecbatana brought them to Meshed, where Satibarzanes, governor of Aria, met him, imparting

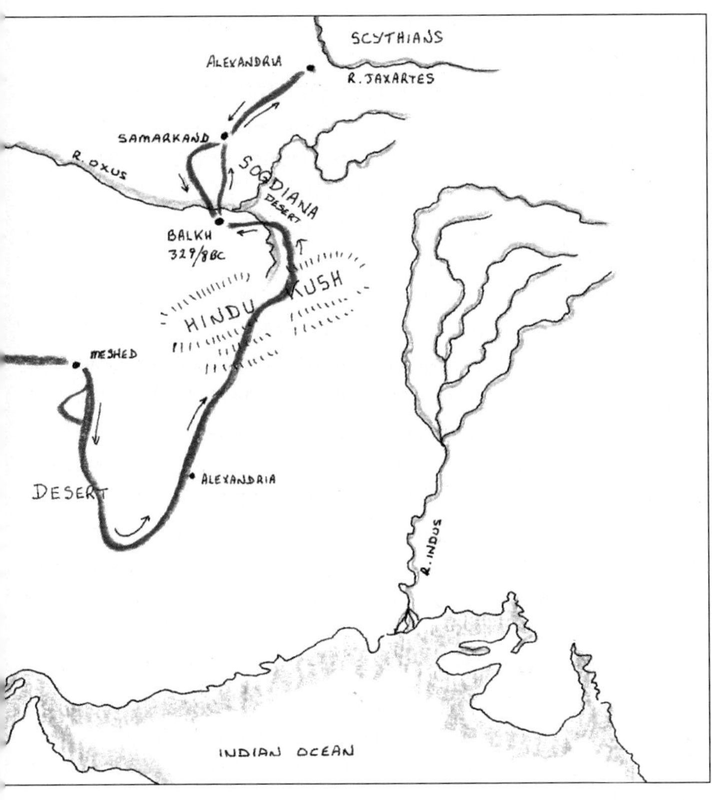

Alexander in Persia (331 - 328 BC).

the news that Bessus was calling himself king and was lodged at Balkh, in the heart of Bactria. Alexander, continuing east but needing to hurry, had his troops bring all their excess baggage and load it on to the wagons. When they hesitated at his order to fire the wagons, he put a torch to his own and with this example they followed suit. Now they could move fast, for the country was too rough for anything but pack animals. Then Alexander heard that Satibarzanes had done a political about turn and was heading fast for Balkh to join Bessus. Alexander gave chase, but Satibarzanes fled into the foothills of the Hindu Kush. The news decided Alexander's route, south through desert before turning north east into the mountains.

Through the heat and sand storms of the dry, barren terrain the army struggled. It is hard to imagine them, not only animals and fighting men but slaves and women as well as the royal court with its seers, philosophers, historians and priests. At last, thirsty, weary and short of supplies, they made camp at a place called Farah and Alexander learned of a plot to kill him. Philotas, Commander of the King's Comapnions, son of Parmenion, was the chief suspect in the conspiracy. He was tried publicly and put to death. Was his father, Parmenion, party to the plot? Evidently Alexander thought so, for he sent a friend of Parmenion back to Ecbatana, with letters for his officers containing the order for the elderly generals' execution. There was also a forged letter to Parmenion pertaining to come from Philotas. As the general was reading the letter which he thought came from his son, the execution was carried out. The letters of Alexander to his officers, explaining the reason for Parmenion's death, were read out to the troops to forestall a mutiny. The general's men stayed loyal to the King.

It was a Macedonian custom that when a man was found guilty of a crime which required the death penalty, his relations were also put to death. Relations and friends of Parmenion

11.   *They survived on fish and herbs.*

and his son were in fear of their lives until reassured by
Alexander. He needed these officers, but put them together
in a new unit, the "Disorderlies". Their letters home were
censored, the discipline was harsh, but they fought bravely
in battle to overcome their disgrace.
In September of the year 330 Alexander set off towards the
foothills of the Hindu Kush and by November they were high
in the mountains, the way rough and dangerous. The army,
stumbling through thick snow and ice, found shelter where
they could, usually in the huts of the natives, which lay low
in the ground, only the rounded roofs showing above the
snow. Through the numbing cold, Alexander led the way,
turning back often to help the men who slipped or felt they
could not go on, for he knew that Bessus would not expect
them to march in winter. When at last the army stumbled

into a valley, Alexander allowed the exhausted men a three month rest. There he founded a city and it was called - Alexandria.

The spring thaw came and the army was back in the mountains. The snow had melted but by the time Alexander and his men descended the slopes in early June, they had eaten some of their horses, food had been so short. Most of the time they had survived on wild herbs and fish caught from mountain streams.

 News of the approaching army reached Bessus in Balkh. At the same time, he heard that his supporter, Satibarzanes, had been killed by a group led by Artabazus, whose daughter, Barsine, if you remember, was Alexander's mistress. Bessus fled, north to the river Oxus, which he crossed, burning his boats behind him.

 Alexander's army by then numbered about 30,000. They had followed him over rivers, across burning deserts, over snow clad mountains and lived on herbs, fish and their own animals. Alexander had shared in their hardships. They followed him after Bessus, into a stony land, the desert of Sogdiana.

They slept through the burning heat of the day, when the sand shimmered with the heat haze and mirages gave false images of beautiful cities rising out of cool lakes. Travelling by night, stumbling through the darkness, over rocks or knee deep in sand, in their thirst they drank all their water in the first few days. A great many men were lost. When Alexander was brought some water by men who had gone ahead to establish a camp, he refused to drink, pouring it away, because his men were thirsty. On reaching the camp, he ordered fires to be lit, to guide the stragglers, refusing food and drink until all his men were safe.

The wide river Oxus was crossed in the same way as Alexander had crossed the Danube, by stitching the leather tents together and stuffing them with straw to make rafts. This great army, 30,000 armed men, cavalry horses, pack animals, supply wagons, elephants also, captives, wives, probably children and certainly an assorment of the usual camp followers, made the crossing on home made rafts. They were over the river in five days, but once more Alexander was frustrated in his desire to do battle with an enemy. Bessus was the victim of a plot. He had been seized and taken to a village to be handed over to Alexander, who sent Ptolemy for him, telling him to treat him like a common criminal. Alexander found him naked and bound at the side of the road. He was flogged and sent in chains to Artabazus in Balkh, to await his fate.

The boundary of the Persian empire to the north lay at the Jaxartes river and Alexander marched on, wishing to lay claim to the whole kingdom. But his men were hungry and they foraged for food on the way. Local tribes, probably also at starvation point, took exception to this and attacked. Alexander, as usual at the front in the ensuing fracas, suffered an arrow wound to the leg. He had to be carried in a litter and there was much arguing about who should bear the burden to Samarkand and the king suggested they should take turns. His wound not yet healed, Alexander left 1,000 troops to defend Samarkand and continued to the frontier where he ordered the building of a city - Alexandria. Before building could begin, the local people rose in rebellion. Alexander took seven villages. The first three fell to him after a short seige, the next two surrendered but the sixth fought hard and Alexander was severely wounded in the neck when he gained entrance by tunnelling under the walls. In spite of his wound he razed the place to the ground and the seventh village surrendered quickly.

Alexander returned to the building of his city, Alexandria the Furthest, on the banks of the Jaxartes, still suffering from his neck wound and unable to speak above a whisper. It was not a good time for him. He recieved news that his 1,000 troops who held Samarkand were being beseiged. On the other side of the river, the Scythians were massing. Alexander dispatched 2,000 of his men to Samarkand and crossed the river to deal with the Scyths, who were no match for him and they fled, pursued, but not by Alexander, who was sick, either from his wound or from the river water he had drunk.

Returning to Samarkand, Alexander found he had to bury all 2,000 of the men he had sent to relieve the city. Spitamenes, the man responsible, had departed in haste on hearing of Alexander's approach. The king returned to cross the Oxus river and the army wintered in Balkh.

In the spring of 328, Alexander returned to the delightful climate of Samarkand and here the army hunted, capturing 4,000 wild animals in the surrounding woods and forests, the meat being a welcome addition to their larder.

One evening, at a banquet, the king and his companions drank too much wine. It was a Macedonian habit, to drink heavily and although Alexander was drinking more frequently, it was only in his leisure hours. Cleitus, the man who had saved Alexander's life at the battle of the Granicus river, was a guest and he also imbibed heavily. A quarrel broke out. Alexander boasted that he had done greater things than Philip, his father. Cleitus, who had fought with Philip, disagreed. He said that the king's successes were due to Philip's army and generals. Alexander tolerated such jibes for a while but in the end the king lost control of his temper, took up a weapon and killed Cleitus.

As with most great men throughout the ages, Alexander was a man of vigour and passion. These qualities, which worked well for him most of the time, for the second time had got the better of him and, for the second time, wine was partly to blame. This tragedy was worse than the burning of Persepolis, though.

How could he, even the worse for drink and in a rage, have killed such an old friend? His men forgave him, but he could no forgive himself. Cleitus had been the brother of Alexander's nurse, he had been a loyal soldier and the king owed him his life. For three days he lay weeping on his bed refusing to eat, such was his shame and revulsion.

Ten days passed before Alexander had pulled himself together. Spitamenes was still loose and waging a guerilla type warfare. Once more, however, Alexander was cheated of his revenge, for the Scythians turned on Spitamenes, killed him and sent his head to Alexander, although some say that his wife slew him and personally brought his head to the king. But there were more rebels to deal with, Bessus' men, some of whom had locked themselves into a rocky fortress in the mountains, three miles high and impregnable. From there they mocked at Alexander, saying that his army would need to grow wings and fly, to reach them.

Nothing was impregnable to Alexander. He sent 300 men to scale the heights under cover of darkeness, equipped with ropes and iron tent pegs, which they hammered into the rock as they went. Alexander offered twelve talents to the first to reach the top, eleven for the next men and so on. The three hundred who volunteered were expert climbers, nevertheless, thirty men were lost in the ascent

12.   *They captured wild animals.*

and the enemey surrendered when the remaining 270
appeared unexpectedly at the summit, like ghosts in the
early morning mist.
Among the captives from the rock was a beautiful woman,
Roxane, daughter of Oxyartes, a Sogdian lord. Alexander
fell deeply in love with a woman for the first time in his life.
They married at Balkh during the winter of 327 BC.
The Greeks had accepted his wearing of foreign clothes,
his foreign lover and now his foreign wife. But they could
not all accept his next orders. They had to make obeisance
to Alexander. This was a custom called "proskynesis", a
touch of the hand to the mouth accompanied by a deep bow.
It was a gesture of deep respect from an inferior to a superior

and in Greece it was only given to gods. In Persia it was an acceptable practise, proskynesis being paid by the low born to those of nobler birth and always to kings. Perhaps Alexander thought that the Persians may not have believed he was king, if they had seen his own men treating him without the proper respect due.

Macedonians and Greeks alike only had to make a small bow, Persians had to prostrate themselves. However, once introduced, Kallisthenes, his historian, refused to make obeisance. We will hear more about him shortly. For now, there was another plot against the king.

While out hunting, Alexander had chased a wild boar and cornered it. Before he could kill the animal, one of his attendants, a rash young man named Hermolaus, speared the boar and for this, Alexander had him publicly flogged. Smarting after the humiliating experience, Hermolaus hatched a plan, along with his lover and several attendants, to assassinate the king. One of the youths took fright at the last moment and told his brother, who warned Alexander in time. Hermolaus and his companions were put to death and, as Kallisthenes had been their confidante, the king siezed the opportunity and he was executed, although possibly innocent of any crime. Kallisthenes was a nephew of Aristotle, a fact which may be related to future events.

There could well have been some unrest in the army after these events. Alexander knew the best thing to do was to move, quickly, giving the troops something else to occupy their thoughts. He marched into India.

Part 7

India. Battle with Porus, a mutiny and Alexander is wounded.

In early Autumn Alexander led an army of about 50,000 men towards the Indian frontier, where he was met by local rulers who submitted to him. Rajahs from the Indus valley arrived also, putting twenty five elephants at his disposal.

By this time, Alexander's army had very little connection with his father's before him. Parmenion had gone and with him his son Philotas, along with Cleitus. Hephaestion, Ptolemy and Perdicaas, Alexander's greatest friends, led various sections of his forces.

Alexander divided his men, sending Hephaestion and Perdicaas ahead to the river Indus, to prepare for the crossing. He himself took the rest of the men further north, into the Swat hills, putting down small native uprisings, at Andaca and Euaspla as he went.

At Arigaeum, the locals put up a strong defence. When they were finally routed, Alexander was impressed with the many heads of healthy, humped cattle they captured. He picked out the finest and had them sent back to Macedonia for breeding purposes. Theodore Dodge, an American General wrote in 1890 "...this was the origin of the hump still seen on cattle in parts of Greece."

When Alexander and his men came to the city of Nysa and camped for the night, the weather grew cold and the troops looked around for firewood. Running out of logs, they discovered boxes of cedar wood on the hillsides, which made excellent firewood but, unknown to them, were coffins.

The local people were outraged and their leaders came to Alexander's tent. They found him, still dressed in full armour and, dumbstruck at the sight, they fell prostrate before him. When they found their tongues, a deal was struck. Alexander left them in power and they in return supplied him with three hundred men to serve in his cavalry. In the course of conversation, it is said, they told him that Dionysus had been there before him. The troops found ivy and vines growing all over the surrounding hillsides and in their nostalgic longing for home, they were delighted to see these familiar plants which belonged to their god of wine. They wreathed their heads with ivy, singing and dancing in Dionysiac celebration. By March of the year 326 Alexander had reached the hills overlooking the eastern shores of the Indus river, well north of Hephaestion and the rest of his army. They came to a sheer rock, called the Aornas, at the top of which a force of local rebels had posted themselves. On the east side of the rock flowed the Indus, while the other sides were protected by deep ravines. Heracles was said to have been unable

13.   *Elephants were put at Alexander's disposal.*

14.   *Ivy and vines grew on the hillsides.*

to storm Aornas. This would have determined Alexander. He ordered his men to fell the pine trees which grew in the area and, he himself throwing the first piece of timber into the ravine, in six days they had built a mound by which they could cross. But this did not bring them to the summit of the rock. The catapults may have been in range, but Alexander and his men were still some several hundred feet down. Up sheer precipices he and thirty chosen men climbed, only to be showered with rocks and boulders from above. Some, including Alexander, made it to the top but after fierce fighting they had to withdraw. Nevertheless, he made camp, blocked roads, brought his siege equipment close and so the enemy, who on the top of the great rock had water and crops and could have lasted out for many months, lost heart and began to leave one night, by the light of blazing torches. Alexander scaled the heights once more, those rebels left were put to the sword and an altar to Athena was built in thanksgiving. Where Heracles had failed, his men must have thought, Alexander had succeeded.

Spring had arrived once more when Alexander joined Hephaestion at Hund, where his faithful friend had built a bridge across the Indus. Hephaestion and his men had been fed with the grain of the ruler of that area, a certain Omphis who, hearing that Alexander had crossed the river and was approaching, set out to meet him, accompanied by his army and many elephants. To Alexander, from the distance, the approaching forces did not look peaceful. Putting his men at the ready, he rode out ahead to take a closer look and luckily Omphis, unarmed, did the same. The two met and established friendly relations. Omphis presented Alexander with 3,000 bulls, thirty elephants, and great number of sheep. For three days he entertained the Macedonian king, adding silver and gold to his gifts.

In the nearby city of Taxila, Alexander met a sect of wise men called Gymnosophists. They combined gymnastics with philosophy and two of them dined with the king, the younger standing on one leg for most of the time. The older of the two was named Calanus. He had taken a forty-year vow to lead a life of austerity which had come to an end and he joined Alexander, living in his camp for two years and the pair became great friends. When Calanus fell ill in Susa, on Alexander's march for home, he insisted on death, Indian style, rather than a lingering half life. He had a funeral pyre built, climbed on and "did not flinch at the flames". Before his death, taking his farewell of Alexander, he told him he would meet him again, in Babylon.

In the meantime, Alexander's friendship with Omphis

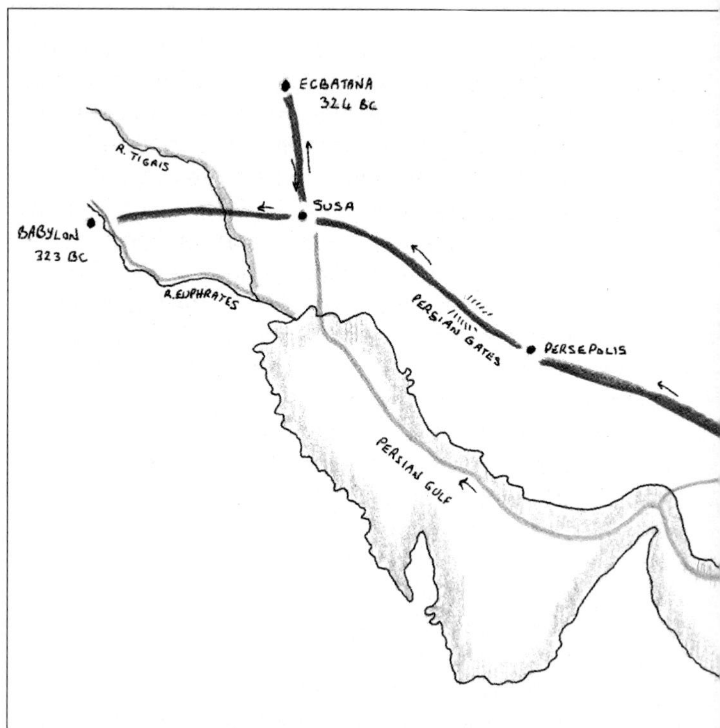

Map 9

produced a new enemy, Porus, whose land lay east of the river Hydaspes, a tributary of the Indus. In May, 326 BC, the two armies faced each other across the river which, after the spring monsoons, was in spate. The rushing waters of the river, which owing to the rains was almost half a mile wide, were a fearful sight, yet not as formidable as the spectacle of Porus and his array of, some say one hundred, some put the number at as many as three hundred, huge

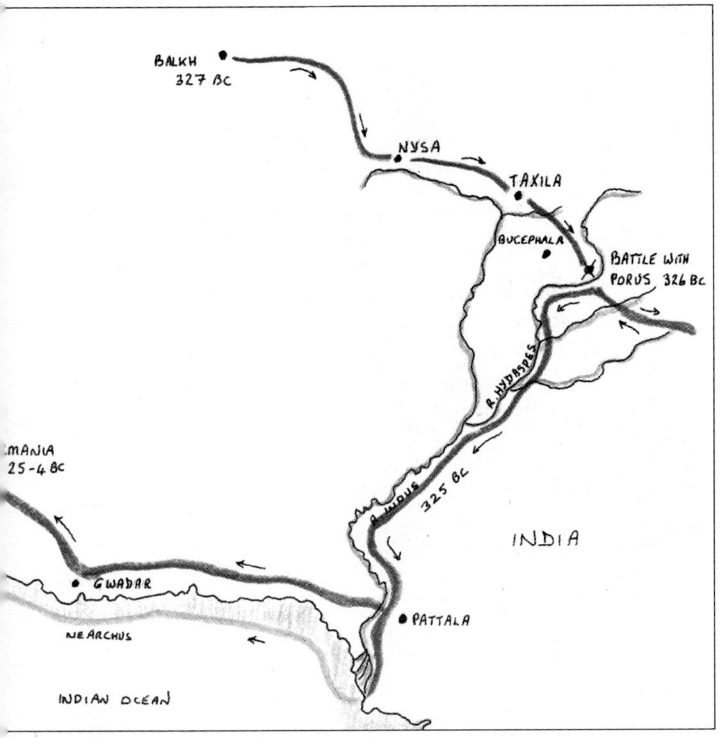

Alexander's journey into India and his return to Babylon 327-323 BC.

elephants. Porus himself, a man of great size, appeared even greater, clad in his armour and seated on the largest elephant of all.

The river was so formidable that even Alexander was unable to cross. So he began a war of intimidation. He brought in stores, to make Porus think he was going to sit things out until the river fell. He sent boats out into the river and then brought them back, appearing hesitant. He sent troops

15.   *The young Alexander on Bucephalus.*

some distance along the shores at night, shouting war cries. When Porus prepared for the expected attack, the men withdrew. Eventually, the game of bluff succeeded and Porus began to ignore Alexander's tactics. The moment had come.

Alexander had noted a sizeable island in the river some miles upstream. It was well wooded, so it would provide cover for his men and on his side there was a headland, behind which he could conceal his forces. Ptolemy acted as decoy further downstream. In Alexander's camp the normal number of fires were lit after sunset while Alexander himself, under cover of darkeness and Lady Luck with him once more in the disguise of a noisy, violent storm, crossed to the island and thence to the opposite bank with his main force. The finer details of the ensuing battle can be read elsewhere, but we can imagine the chaos caused as the mud, thick after the monsoons, was churned up by huge, trumpeting elephants. Chariots were stranded, their wheels deep in the mire. Frightened, rearing horses, drum beats and the cries of the wounded added to the confusion.

The lumbering elephants were, in the end, no match for Alexander's cavalry. When the Macedonians wielded axes, cutting at the feet of the elephants, the great animals went berserk, turned and crushed many of their own Indians underfoot. Porus fought with much courage. When he was wounded and captured, possibly by Alexander who chased him on the faithful Bucephalus, it is said that, impressed by his bravery, the king himself tended his injuries and, when he had recovered, Alexander gave him back his lands and re-instated him as Rajah.

Some say he was wounded in the battle, others that he died of old age and still others that, exhausted during the chase to capture Poros and to avoid throwing the king, he carefully knelt down and died. Whichever story is true though, Alexander's trusty steed, Bucephalas, passed away. Alexander had loved the horse passionately, even, according to Arrian, threatening to kill all the Uxians when the horse was stolen in their land. It was brought back immediately. The king led the funeral procession, buried the remains of his horse and by the river Hydaspes he founded two cities, one named Nicaea, meaning victory, and the other, Bucephala.

Alexander gave orders for wood to be cut for ship building. He had noticed that the crops and wild life around the river were similar to those around the Nile and mistakenly thought that the Indus flowed south west and thence into Egypt. When he had conquered the lands to the east, his plan was to return to the Hydaspes and from there sail to Egypt and Alexandria.

Alexander marched a weary army on, eastwards, through mud and rain. Beyond the next river, he had been told, lay a twelve day journey across barren land to the Ganges and a king whose army numbered 200,000. Another challenge for Alexander. But when they reached the next river, his army refused to go any further. Their spokesman was Coenus, a cavalry commander who had been with Alexander since leaving Macedonia. Alexander pleaded with him, but to no avail. The men were tattered, weary and dispirited. Alexander sulked in his tent for three days before giving way. When he announced that they would turn back, the men could not cheer, but wept for joy. Before they left the area, Alexander had twelve great altars built and held sacrifices, games and feasts. Nor long after they had begun their homeward journey, Coenus died and Alexander buried him with the honours due to a brave and loyal soldier. Back at the Hydaspes river, where Alexander had realised his mistake and knew he could only reach as far as the Euphrates by water, reinforcements from Thrace had arrived, along with new suits of armour and other supplies. With the feeling that they were on their way home, the men threw themselves into the task of ship building with vigour and within weeks they set off, down river, Alexander's friend Nearchus being appointed Admiral.

If the men, however, thought they were done with land battles, they were mistaken. There were several stops on the journey to put down small insurrections and Alexander had heard of a fierce and rebellious tribe, the Malli, which he intended to search out and subdue. But before he could do so, the fleet rounded a bend in the river and were confronted with roaring rapids. The lighter ships were soon out of control and even the king had to swim for his life to shore.

Leaving the repairs to his fleet underway, Alexander took a select band of men and went in search of the Malli, marching overnight through desert land and surprising many tribesmen in their fields. They mowed many down while others fled to take refuge behind the great double walls of their capital city. His men were reluctant to face another battle but after Alexander's pleas and exhorations, the weary soldiers once more committed themselves. The seige equipment was brought up to the walls and Alexander was first to reach the battlements, where he got cut off from his men as the ladders broke. Fighting off his attackers, he jumped down into the city. With his back against a tree he fought for his life while his forces outside, with renewed courage, battled their way in to the city in time to save their king, but not before he had been severely wounded. None of the inhabitants of the city were spared. Men, women and children were massacred.

Alexander's wound was a serious one. A barbed arrow had pierced a lung and he was not expected to live. The arrow was removed, causing haemorrhage and the king lost

16.

consciousness. Credit must be given to both his medical treatment and his tough constitution, for he lived.
Rumours that the king was dead reached the main army. After a week, although his wound was still not healed, Alexander had himself placed in a ship and taken back to

Ships with richly coloured sails.

join the fleet. When the men saw him, alive, the very woods nearby, it was said, echoed with their cheering.
During Alexander's weeks of convalescence, local Indians sent gifts of pearls and tortoise shells, linen, lizard skins, lions and tigers. The king gave a sumptuous feast for the

rajahs, setting one hundred golden sofas around the laden tables. Slowly his health improved. He sent his older soldiers, the wounded, elephants and some infantry along the road to Susa, under the leadership of Craterus. He himself sailed on down the Indus. When they reached the open sea, Nearchus was to sail the fleet up to the mouth of the Euphrates and he would march along the coast with the main army, thus able to provide for the fleet along the way.

As the great flotilla of ships with its richly coloured sails accompanied by the splashing of oars and murmur of voices, made its way down the river, the sight struck terror into the hearts of the tribes who lived along its banks.

Most of them surrendered, to willingly provision the fleet but occasionally Alexander had to resort to arms, at one point losing many men, for the Indians had smeared poison on their swords.

Towards the middle of July, 325, the fleet reached Pattala. The occupants had fled, so Alexander was able to take on board grain and cattle in plenty before continuing towards the mouth of the Indus and the open sea.

There is very little noticeable tide in the land locked Mediterranean and suddenly, as the fleet sailed down one arm of the delta, the men were surprised to meet a fast incoming flow of water. Chaos reigned but it was nothing to the panic caused when, some hours later, they found themselves stranded by the ebb tide. When the sea flowed back and they found themselves afloat once more, although some damage had been done, they began to understand the strange phenomenon and sacrificed to Poseidon, the god of the sea, in thanksgiving.

Part 8

The weary march home, weddings, farewell to Hephaestion and the death of Alexander.

From the Indus the army set out, but not before Alexander had to borrow money from his friends, for provisions. We do not know why his treasury was empty at this point. His secretary, Eumenes, who had been Philip's secretary also, refused to give as much as the others and Alexander set fire to his tent, just to watch him save his valuables. He was not as poor as he had made out. For some reason, we are told, Hephaestion hated Eumenes.

The army marched parallel with the coast, for they needed to keep a link with Nearchus and the fleet. The idea was that the army would carry the grain and other provisions for the fleet and would dig wells as they marched, to supply the ships with fresh water.

Alexander, it is said, was "aware of the difficulties" of his journey, but his luck soon deserted him for the supplies he had ordered to be stationed along the route never materialised. As for the fleet, unknown to Alexander, after he departed the monsoon winds blew and kept Nearchus in harbour for three months. So when, after some weeks of marching, the king reached the Makran desert, they had no contact with the fleet and had run out of supplies. The land through which they marched had never been crossed. Although they travelled at night, temperatures remained high in the barren, dry desert. Wild animals and insects proliferated. The carts could not negotiate the great undulating dunes of fine, sifting sand. Many died of thirst. When the rains finally came, they camped by a stream. The women and children were closest to the water's edge when, in the early hours of the morning, a flash flood swept most of them away and they drowned, along with many pack animals and the royal tent. Alexander was safe, as he had risen before dawn.

The army was starving. As the animals died, they were eaten and soon many were being helped to their final end deliberately. Poisonous plants and snakes added to the discomfort and disease as well as hunger caused the death of many. A sandstorm blew and the guides lost their way. Alexander took a handful of men, rode towards the sea and was lucky to find drinking water. When the guides realised they were near Gwaddar, Alexander and the tattered remains of his army reluctantly left Nearchus to his fate and turned inland, where the going was easier and sheep and goats grazed. On arriving in Karmania where supplies, including wine, were abundant, Alexander made camp, rested the men and feasted.

But what of Nearchus and his fleet? Not only had they had to wait three months at the mouth of the Indus while the monsoons raged, even when they sailed they had five weeks delay not far up the coast, due to unfavourable winds. They were not truly on their way until November. They were soon short of food and water. They survived by raiding coastal villages and taking the meagre flocks. They saw their first whales. In the Straits of Hormuz, the pilots pointed out the promontory of Ras Mussendam and told Nearchus of the spices, including the rare and precious cinammon, which were imported there, from Arabia. At last, after passing the Straits, a favourable wind blew them to friendly shores

17.   *The king celebrated with games.*

where some ventured inland and met a Greek. With joy, they discovered that Alexander was not far away.

When Alexander and Nearchus met, in the capital of Karmania, each was overjoyed and the king celebrated with games and a festival of music.

News arrived of uprisings and revolts in Alexander's widespread Persian empire. He had been away, in India, for many months and some thought him dead. Greeks had rebelled in Bactria. There was trouble in the mountains of the Hindu Kush and Craterus arrived, not only with the veterans, elehants and the king's wife, Roxane, who was soon pregnant, but also with prisoners taken on his route, men who had tried to sieze power from the governors of the hill tribes. Alexander dealt with those before Hephaestion was ordered to Susa with the main army, Nearchus continued his journey towards the mouth of the Euphrates and the king rode for Pasargadae, near Persepolis, where he hanged a certain Braxis, who had made himself ruler.

At Pasargadae was the tomb of Cyrus the Great, founder of the Persian Empire. The king, always appreciative of strength and courage, visited the grave, only to discover that it had been desecrated. He organised the repairs and put the perpetrator to death. The local governor marched with Alexander to Persepolis but was executed there for the crimes of plunder and murder. Alexander continued to Susa, where he imprisoned the governor and put his son to death, for bribery.

The mother of Darius was still in Susa, with her grandchildren. The two girls were old enough to marry. Alexander arranged a great wedding feast in an attempt to unite Persians and Macedonians. He married one sister and Hephaestion the other. His officers were married at the same time to Persian girls of noble birth. A hall containing one hundred bridal suites was built and the feast lasted for five days, held in front of the palace where a great tent was erected, supported with gilded columns.

It was at this time that Alexander received news of Harpalus' defection, to Athens, with a force of mercenary soldiers and an abundance of treasure from Babylon acquired in Alexander's absence. When the messengers brought the king this distressing news about a childhood friend, he did not believe it and imprisoned them. But they were released when he received confirmation of the story.

Perhaps the news from Athens caused Alexander to attend

to Greek matters. In the city states of Greece, there had always been much political in-fighting. When one group took over, the leaders of the outgoing faction were exiled. After several centuries, the land was full of men, or families of men, banished from their homes in this fashion. Many roamed Greece, some had become mercenaries in Darius' army.

Alexander ordered the return, with immunity, of these people and had the Decree of Exiles read out at the 324 BC Olympic Games, to the accompaniment of great cheers. The idea was not welcome to all, however. For many it meant accepting those families, and their descendants, who had been their sworn enemies for a long time.

In Athens they were debating whether to treat Alexander as a god. Demosthenes is recorded as saying that he could be called the son of Zeus for all he cared. In the end, the city decided to humour Alexander and envoys set out to greet him as divine. Also in Athens, a certain Leosthenes hoped to take advantage of Alexander's order for the disbanding of mercenary armies in Persia. These soldiers gathered at Memphis and Leosthenes brought 50,000 of them to the Greek mainland by ship. He would use them in a rebellion.

The 30,000 young Persians, enrolled to train in the ways of the Macedonian soldier some five years before, were now eighteen years old. They arrived in Susa wearing Macedonian dress, drilling expertly, bearing Macedonian weapons, to the annoyance of the Macedonians, especially Alexander's oldest soldiers. When these veterans, ordered to rendezvous with Alexander at Opis, on the river Tigris, were told to go home, it was the last straw. To these old men, who had been with Alexander from the beginning, it was an insult to have their place taken, as they saw it, by young Persians.

When Alexander stood on a platform, saying his farewells and offering them bonus payments, all the Macedonians mutinied, saying that if the elderly were dismissed, then they too were dismissed. The king immediately jumped down, into their midst, marked out the ringleaders and had them arrested and put to death. Alexander next shut himself into his tent and refused to speak to anyone. After two or three days he announced that his decision stood. In fact they could all go. He would have Persian Companions, Shield Bearers and cavalry. Alexander had called their bluff. Two days later, they threw down their weapons outside the king's tent and begged to be allowed in.

Alexander stepped outside his tent, weeping. He kissed them all, saying they were his kin and, as they took up their weapons again joyfully, he announced a banquet. Nine thousand, Persians as well as Macedonians, attended the feast and shortly afterwards 10,000 veterans returned, this time willingly and well paid, to their homeland, under the leadership of the faithful Craterus. Craterus was ordered to take over in Macedonia from Antipater, who was to bring Alexander re-inforcements.

Alexander made for Ecbatana. He travelled slowly in the summer heat, arriving in the Autumn and everyone relaxed, the king organising sacrifices to the gods, games and festivities.

Hephaestion caught a fever and after a week of illness, seemed to rally. Alexander was watching a boy's race when the news came that his old friend's condition had worsened. He hurried to his bedside but arrived too late. Hephaestion was dead. It is said that Alexander had his friend's doctor crucified and some say there was a rumour of foul play and that suspicion fell on Eumenes, Alexander's secretary,

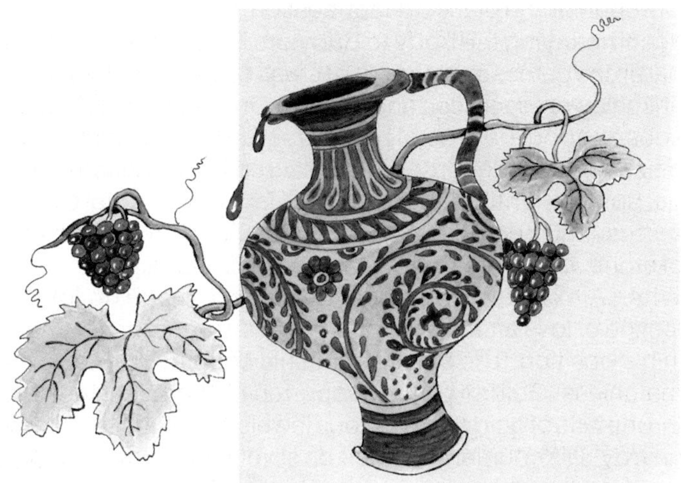

18.   *The wine was poured generously.*

who was known to harbour a grudge against Hephaestion, but he cleared his name by dedicating himself and his armour to the dead man.

Alexander was inconsolable. He could not be torn away from the body. For three days and nights he could not be persuaded to eat or drink. Achilles had torn out his hair when his beloved Patroclus had been killed. Alexander cut his off. It was two weeks before he could make any decision about the funeral and, in the meantime, he sent a deputation to the shrine of Zeus Ammon at Siwa, to request divine honours for Hephaestion. All those who had taken part in the games and festivities before Hephaestion's death were summoned for the funeral games to be held in Babylon.

Perdicaas, who became the Commander of the King's

Companions in place of Hephaestion, was given the task of accompanying the body to Babylon. Three thousand took part in the games and no expense was spared. Ten thousand animals were sacrificed and roasted. On a platform 220 yards square stood the funeral pyre, two hundred feet high. As it blazed, Alexander ordered the sacred fire in the temple to be put out, until the funeral was over. The king built a permanent memorial to Hephaestion; a great lion, carved of stone, it stands in the desert near Ecbatana.

When Alexander recovered, perhaps to make up for the feeling of loss after his friend's death, he began to luxuriate in his position. The splendour of his court at Babylon was matchless. Golden pillars supported his oppulent tent, his throne was of gold and precious jewels and incense burned nearby. His courtiers reclined on silver footed sofas and his guards were splendidly dressed in scarlet, blue and gold. White horses pulled his chariot, libations were poured to him and sacrifices made in his honour. It was said that at dinner parties, where wine was poured generously, he often dressed up as a god and even, at times, as a goddess.

Envoys arrived at his court from all over the world, all wondering what his future intentions were, for Alexander was improving the harbour and building warships. He was looking to Arabia, for ever since Nearchus had talked of spices, the idea had been at the back of his mind to develop the spice trade. He had already sent four men to trace the route back to its source.

So, the harbour improved and ships built, the troops were trained diligently and the growing fleet excercised, the ships competing with each other, racing for trophies.

In the king's apartments, a commoner seated himself on the royal throne. He was arrested and tortured, but he could only say that he simply felt like sitting there. The king's seers decided that this was a bad omen and when Alexander, out in a boat, lost his royal diadem and the sailor who retrieved it absent mindedly placed it on his own head, the seers warned the king of disaster. Horoscopes were cast and his fortune tellers grew alarmed. The future did not bode well.

A ceremony was held, on the 29th May, when Nearchus was given charge of the Arabian expedition which was due to leave on the 4th of June. Afterwards Alexander attended another party, given by one of his Companions, Medius.

What happend afterwards is a mystery. It is agreed that Alexander got very drunk at Medius' party. Some say he collapsed with a fever. Eumenes was at the party. There is one story that the king was poisoned with water from the river Styx.

The waters of the river Styx, according to Pausanias, once meant death to any goat which drank them. The water, he wrote, dissolved glass, crystal, pearl, stone, even diamonds. It destroyed bone, rusted iron, bronze, silver and gold. The only thing incorruptible by the river was a horse's hoof. Kassander, Antipater's son, had arrived from Macedoneia and was at Medius'party. The story is told that he brought the Styx water in a horse's hoof, at Aristotle's instigation, and gave it to Alexander.

There had been previous plots to kill Alexander, but he could well have drunk some local water and contracted typhus. He was ill for ten days and at the end his men demanded to see him. They filed past his bed, but he was too weak to speak to them. He gave Perdicaas his ring. On June the 10th, 323 BC, Alexander the Great died.

19. *Kassander with the horse's hoof*

Part 9

The aftermath

On hearing of the death of their king, Persians and Macedonians alike mourned. When night fell, no-one dared light the lamps and the city of Babylon lay in darkness. Persians shaved their heads and when Sisgambis, mother of Darius, heard the news, she tore out her hair and grieved so much that after five days she was dead.

Roxane's baby had not yet been born. Barsine, Alexander's mistress, had a three year old boy, Heracles. Perdicaas was the possessor of Alexander's ring. A quarrel broke out over the succession.

Perdicaas voted for Roxane's child, as yet unborn. No-one considered Heracles. Meleager, an infantry commander, was for Alexander's half brother, the slow witted Arrhidaeus. Eventually Arrhideaus was put in as ruler, under the guidance of Perdicaas, while all waited for Roxane to give birth. Roxane, meanwhile, sent for her nearest rival, Darius' daughter, whom the king had married in Babylon, and poisoned her. Roxane had a son, Alexander, and the baby was put under Perdicaas' guardianship, but three years later, Perdicaas was dead. Ptolemy became governor of Egypt. Later he became King and Ptolemies ruled Egypt for nearly three hundred years. Meanwhile, the embalmed body of Alexander lay in Babylon and it was said that he had asked to be buried at Siwa. The Macedonian kings, however, had always been buried at Aegae (Modern day Vergina), in Macedonia. The building of his funeral chariot, in which the body would be taken back to Macedonia, took two years. The coffin was gold, overlaid with purple cloth rich in gold embroidery. Over this lay Alexander's shield and helmet. From the coffin rose a great carved canopy, 360 feet high, supported by gilded columns, its friezes painted with scenes depicting Alexander and the whole hung about with curtains, tassells and bells. Sixty four mules pulled the chariot, their harness bejewelled and heads crowned with gold. People came from far and wide to marvel at it.

The funeral procession left Babylon, but was destined never to reach Macedonia. Ptolemy set out from Egypt with an army, met the cortege and escorted it, not to Aegae, nor even to Siwa, but to Memphis. There the great chariot lay, while a tomb was built at Alexandria, where it was seen by many, including the emperor Augustus, three hundred years later. It is possible Marcus Aurleius visited the tomb but there is no record of it ever being seen again.

In Athens, Leosthenes put the Greek mercenaries to use, those that he had brought out of Persia and he led a rebellion against Antipater, instigated by Athens and supported by Argos, Epidauros, Sikyon, Troizen, and many others but not the Boeotians, who held the ruined Thebes and were frightened that Athens might recolonise her. But Leosthenes died, and the rebellion failed.

 Antipater, Alexander's viceroy, died of old age in 319. Macedonians entered and occupied Athens and Olympias, Alexander's mother, came over from Epirus and murdered Arrhidaeus in 317 along with many of the family and friends of Antipater's son, Kassander. She ruled for a time but was defeated by Kassander and handed over to to a mob to be stoned to death.

Kassander murdered Alexander's sons. Heracles was Barsine's child and Alexander IV was Roxane's. They were poisoned. Kassander restored Thebes in 315. He had brought home those Thebans who had been uprooted by Alexander and reached Athens.

When Christianity spread throughout Egypt, the early Christians desecrated the temples, removing the faces of pagan gods. Could the priests of Zeus Ammon have secretly removed Alexander from his resting place in Alexandria and taken it to Siwa for safety? Did Ptolemy give Alexander his last wish and bury him at Siwa, substituting his body before it left Memphis for Alexandria? Will we ever know? And what of those who thought he was divine? Parmenion, a Greek poet wrote,

"The rumour's false that Alexander's dead,

Unless we hold that Phoebus told a lie:

"Thou art invincible,' the Pythian said;

And those that are invincible can't die".

There is more than one way to be immortal. The legends of Alexander live on.

Ends

CHRONOLOGY

359 BC	Philip ascends throne.
357	Philip marries Olympias.
356	20th July, Alexander is born.
338	2nd August, Battle of Chaeronea.
336	Summer - Phlip dies, Alexander's accession.
336 / 5	Deaths of those who plotted against the throne, including Attalus and Amyntas.
335	Thebes is destroyed.
334	Alexander crosses the Hellespont, wins Battle of Granicus river. Sardis, Miletus and Halicarnassus fall to him.
334 / 3	Winter, Lycia and Pamphylia fall and Memnon dies.
333	Spring, Alexander cuts the Gordium knot. Summer, Alexander falls ill. November, Battle of Issus. Winter, Alexander takes Sidon.
332	January, seige of Tyre.
332	September, seige of Gaza.
332 / 1	Winter, Alexander goes to Siwa.
331	Spring, Egypt and the founding of Alexandria.
331	Autumn, eclipse of the moon on the 20th September, followed by Battle of Guagamela. Alexander enters Babylon and Susa.
330	Spring, Persepolis burns.
330	July, death of Darius, trial and execution of Philotas, execution of Parmenion.

330 / 29	Death of Satibarzanes, Bessus murdered.
329	Summer, Spitamenes rebels.
329 / 8	Winter in Balkh.
328 / 7	Death of Cleitus, Spitamenes loses his head. Sogdians defeated on the rock. Alexander marries Roxane. Introduction of Proskyneisis, execution of Hermolaus and Kallisthenes.
327 / 6	Winter, Alexander in the Swat hills, capture of rebels on Aornus.
326	Spring, Battle with Porus. Death of Bucephalus.
326	Summer, Mutiny, Death of Coenus.
326/5	Winter, descent of the Indus river and Alexander is seriously wounded.
325	Summer, Alexander begins his coastal march home.
325 / 4	Winter, Alexander in Karmania, punishment of the local governors.
324	Summer, The Exiles Decree read at the Olympic Games. Meeting and mutiny at Opis.
324	Autumn, death of Hephaestion.
323	Spring, May 29th, Medius gives a dinner party and Alexander falls ill.
323	10th June Alexander's death. The political settlement at Babylon.
321	Alexander's body taken to Egypt.
319	Death of Antipater.
317	Arrhidaeus and Antipater's family murdered.
315	Thebes restored by Kassander.

Index

— A —

— B —

— C —

— D —

— E —

— J —

— K —

— L —

— M —

— N —

— S —

— T —

— V —

— X —

— Z —

Bibliography

The History of Alexander. Quintus Curtius Rufus. Interesting but emotional, full of rhetoric and moralising.

Alexander the Great. Robin Lane Fox. Detailed, erudite and imaginative.

Alexander. Theodore Ayrault Dodge. Detailed descriptions of warfare.

The Nature of Alexander. Emotional, romantic but scholarly.

The Iliad. Homer. Alexander's favourite work.

Xenophon. Anabisis & Cyropaedia. Alexander must have read both.